W9-BED-411

GENDER IDENTITY
THE SEARCH FOR SELF

By Kate Light

Published in 2017 by
Lucent Press, an Imprint of Greenhaven Publishing, LLC
353 3rd Avenue
Suite 255
New York, NY 10010

Designer: Deanna Paternostro
Editor: Jennifer Lombardo

Cataloging-in-Publication Data

Names: Light, Kate.
Title: Gender Identity: The Search for Self / Kate Light.
Description: New York : Lucent Press, 2017. | Series: Hot Topics | Includes index.
Identifiers: ISBN 9781534560239 (library bound) | ISBN 9781534560246 (ebook)
Subjects: LCSH: Transgender people–Juvenile literature. | Transgender people–Identity–Juvenile literature. | Gender identity–Juvenile literature.
Classification: LCC HQ77.9 L38 2017 | DDC 305.3–dc23

Printed in the United States of America

CPSIA compliance information: Batch #CW17KL: For further information contact Greenhaven Publishing LLC, New York, New York at 1-844-317-7404.

Please visit our website, www.greenhavenpublishing.com. For a free color catalog of all our high-quality books, call toll free 1-844-317-7404 or fax 1-844-317-7405.

CONTENTS

A dolescence is a time when many people begin to take notice of the world around them. News channels, blogs, and talk radio shows are constantly promoting one view or another; very few are unbiased. Young people also hear conflicting information from parents, friends, teachers, and acquaintances. Often, they will hear only one side of an issue or be given flawed information. People who are trying to support a particular viewpoint may cite inaccurate facts and statistics on their blogs, and news programs present many conflicting views of important issues in our society. In a world where it seems everyone has a platform to share their thoughts, it can be difficult to find unbiased, accurate information about important issues.

It is not only facts that are important. In blog posts, in comments on online videos, and on talk shows, people will share opinions that are not necessarily true or false, but can still have a strong impact. For example, many young people struggle with their body image. Seeing or hearing negative comments about particular body types online can have a huge effect on the way someone views himself or herself and may lead to depression and anxiety. Although it is important not to keep information hidden from young people under the guise of protecting them, it is equally important to offer encouragement on issues that affect their mental health.

The titles in the Hot Topics series provide readers with different viewpoints on important issues in today's society. Many of these issues, such as teen pregnancy and Internet safety, are of immediate concern to young people. This series aims to give readers factual context on these crucial topics in a way that lets them form their own opinions. The facts presented throughout also serve to empower readers to help themselves or support people they know who are struggling with many of the challenges adolescents face today. Although negative viewpoints are not ignored or downplayed, this series allows young people to see that the challenges they face are not insurmountable. Eating disorders can be overcome, the Internet can be navigated safely, and pregnant teens do not have to feel hopeless.

Quotes encompassing all viewpoints are presented and cited so readers can trace them back to their original source, verifying for themselves whether the information comes from a reputable place. Additional books and websites are listed, giving readers a starting point from which to continue their own research. Chapter questions encourage discussion, allowing young people to hear and understand their classmates' points of view as they further solidify their own. Full-color photographs and enlightening charts provide a deeper understanding of the topics at hand. All of these features augment the informative text, helping young people understand the world they live in and formulate their own opinions concerning the best way they can improve it.

A Long History of Discrimination

Western society has always left out the narratives of minority and oppressed groups throughout its history. In recent years, stories of transgender, nonbinary, gender nonconforming, and intersex individuals have finally begun to reach a wider audience through mainstream media. These individuals and communities have always existed, but society is only just beginning to understand their experiences and struggles. This progress is long overdue, and there is still much work that needs to be done so transgender, nonbinary, gender nonconforming, and intersex individuals can live freely and openly, enjoying the same privileges cisgender people have come to take for granted.

A 2016 survey by The Williams Institute found that 1.4 million adults identify as transgender in the United States. As of 2016, there have been no surveys to determine how many of America's youth identify as transgender, nonbinary, or gender nonconforming. However, there are some studies that give an idea of the number of youth with gender identities other than cisgender. Dane County, Wisconsin's 2015 Youth Assessment Overview surveyed 18,494 high school students, and 1.5 percent identified themselves as transgender. In a survey of 1,032 high school students in Boston, Massachusetts, 1.6 percent identified as transgender, 6.3 percent answered that they did not know, and 5.7 percent skipped the question. These youth and adults deserve to have their voices heard by society and the equality that the transgender community has historically been denied.

This book will introduce readers to essential knowledge about sex, gender identity, and gender expression in Western society with a focus on the United States. As these are all deeply personal topics, there are many areas of differing opinions. The intention of this book is to provide readers access to research and information on the transgender community so they can form their own understanding of gender identity. Many of the terms that appear in this book have multiple definitions or can mean different things to different individuals. Some of these terms may be considered appropriate by some and offensive by others. Furthermore, language that is appropriate today may be considered offensive in the future as society continues to evolve and gain a better understanding of gender identity.

TIMELINE OF SIGNIFICANT MOMENTS IN THE TRANSGENDER COMMUNITY'S HISTORY

1952
Christine Jorgensen's medical transition spreads awareness of the transgender community. She becomes the first widely known transgender individual in the United States.

1964
Philanthropist Reed Erickson creates the Erickson Educational Foundation after transitioning in 1963. He donates millions of dollars toward equality for gay and transgender individuals.

1966
Transgender women protest against discrimination and police harassment during the Compton Cafeteria Riots.

1969
Transgender leaders Marsha P. Johnson, Sylvia Rivera, and other transgender and gender nonconforming individuals join the Stonewall Riots. This was the birth of the Gay Liberation Front and other LGBTQIA civil rights organizations and is largely considered one of history's first major protests for LGBTQIA rights.

1970
Sylvia Rivera and Marsha P. Johnson create the Street Transvestite Action Revolutionaries (STAR), an advocacy group and shelter in New York.

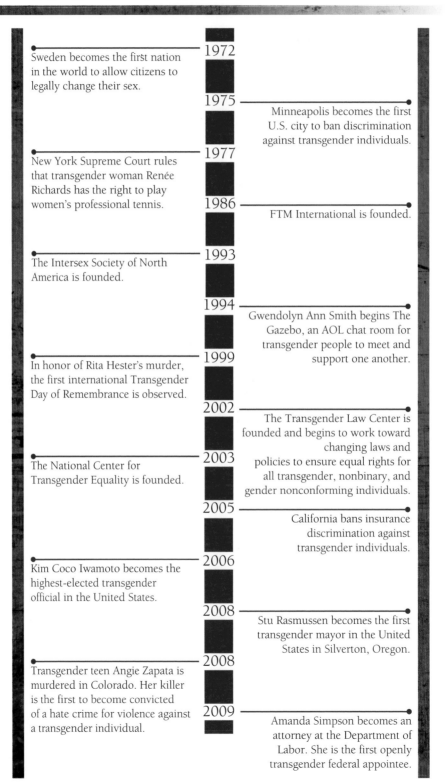

1972
Sweden becomes the first nation in the world to allow citizens to legally change their sex.

1975
Minneapolis becomes the first U.S. city to ban discrimination against transgender individuals.

1977
New York Supreme Court rules that transgender woman Renée Richards has the right to play women's professional tennis.

1986
FTM International is founded.

1993
The Intersex Society of North America is founded.

1994
Gwendolyn Ann Smith begins The Gazebo, an AOL chat room for transgender people to meet and support one another.

1999
In honor of Rita Hester's murder, the first international Transgender Day of Remembrance is observed.

2002
The Transgender Law Center is founded and begins to work toward changing laws and policies to ensure equal rights for all transgender, nonbinary, and gender nonconforming individuals.

2003
The National Center for Transgender Equality is founded.

2005
California bans insurance discrimination against transgender individuals.

2006
Kim Coco Iwamoto becomes the highest-elected transgender official in the United States.

2008
Stu Rasmussen becomes the first transgender mayor in the United States in Silverton, Oregon.

2008
Transgender teen Angie Zapata is murdered in Colorado. Her killer is the first to become convicted of a hate crime for violence against a transgender individual.

2009
Amanda Simpson becomes an attorney at the Department of Labor. She is the first openly transgender federal appointee.

2010

Phyllis R. Frye becomes the first openly transgender judge in the United States, followed shortly by Victoria Kolakowski, who becomes the first openly transgender trial judge.

2012

The Equal Employment Opportunity Commission explicitly protects transgender employees.

2012

The Girl Scouts of Colorado publicly welcome all children who identify as girls to join.

2014

The Department of Health and Human Services reverses a Medicare policy that had been practiced since 1981. Medicare now must cover gender-affirming procedures and treatments.

2014

Laverne Cox becomes the first openly transgender person to appear on the cover of *TIME* magazine.

2015

Leelah Alcorn's suicide sparks a petition for Leelah's Law, which calls for a federal ban of conversion therapy.

2015

Facebook allows users to customize their gender markers.

2015

Caitlyn Jenner comes out as transgender.

2015

Jazz Jennings's reality television show, *I Am Jazz*, premieres.

2015

Governor Andrew M. Cuomo announces an executive order to prohibit discrimination against transgender individuals.

2015

Congress holds its first forum on transgender life in the United States and launches a task force dedicated to transgender rights.

2016

Chelsea Manning, a U.S. prisoner, is approved for gender-affirming surgery.

2016

Sarah McBride, national press secretary for the Human Rights Campaign, is the first openly transgender person to address the Democratic National Conference.

2016

The Pentagon lifts its ban on transgender people serving in the military.

CHAPTER 1

What Is Sex?

Expecting mothers are often asked the question, "Is it a boy or a girl?" This seemingly simple question reveals many of the assumptions people make about sex and gender as a society. They assume that humans are biologically divided into "female" and "male" categories, and that all infants are born with anatomy that is either entirely "female" or entirely "male." They assume that an infant's anatomy will determine how they choose to express themselves throughout their lifetime, and in believing this, they assume that sex and gender mean the same thing.

Society's ideas about gender are rooted in its traditional ideas about anatomy. This has constructed the belief that human bodies come in only two forms: female and male. The gender binary builds on this belief by outlining which behaviors and appearances are "feminine" and which are "masculine." In reality, sex and gender are both far more complex than society acknowledges.

Assigned Sex

Doctors assign a sex to an infant at birth, generally based only on the appearance of the baby's genitals. Infants with vaginas are designated female, and infants with penises are designated male. Most medical and scientific organizations refer to a person's genitals as their "biological sex." However, many people find this term offensive because it oversimplifies the complexities of sex and gender. "Assigned sex" or "designated sex" are largely considered more appropriate, but it is a matter of individual choice. This book will use "assigned sex" to refer to the sex an infant is labeled as at birth.

An infant's assigned sex determines their assigned gender. People often confuse these two terms because society links them so closely together. However, they refer to different aspects of a person's identity and the terms cannot be used interchangeably.

A person's assigned sex is a label given to their anatomy. Assigned gender influences how a person is perceived and treated by their family, friends, and society. This is because the gender binary operates on the belief that our anatomy determines many aspects of our personalities, abilities, interests, and identities. However, human anatomy is much more complex than this binary acknowledges. When a closer look is taken at sex and its many variations, it becomes evident how society has artificially created the link between sex and gender.

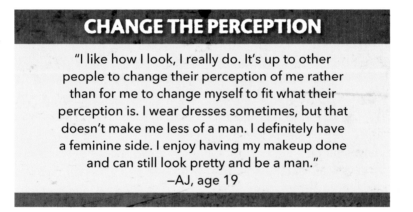

CHANGE THE PERCEPTION

"I like how I look, I really do. It's up to other people to change their perception of me rather than for me to change myself to fit what their perception is. I wear dresses sometimes, but that doesn't make me less of a man. I definitely have a feminine side. I enjoy having my makeup done and can still look pretty and be a man."

–AJ, age 19

Quoted in David Yi, "The Faces of Transgender Teen America," Mashable, July 15, 2015. mashable.com/2015/08/31/transgender-teenagers/#2MZ4gdWPskql.

Sex is actually defined by four primary characteristics and many secondary characteristics that develop during puberty. During puberty, people develop secondary sex characteristics such as facial hair, breasts, and vocal changes. Primary sex characteristics include genitals (external), sex organs (internal), hormones (secreted by glands), and chromosomes (part of a person's DNA).

Human beings typically have 46 chromosomes, which are grouped into 23 pairs. Scientists refer to the 23rd pair as sex chromosomes, and they generally come in two forms: X and Y. Most people

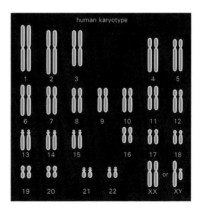

Karyotypes show a person's chromosomes. The 23rd pair, sex chromosomes, differ from person to person. There are many variations of sex chromosomes.

are born with either XX chromosomes or XY chromosomes. These pairs are associated with different traits. The majority of people with XX chromosomes are born with and later develop sex traits which society considers "female," while the majority of people with XY chromosomes are born with and develop sex traits which society considers "male." One of the most common misconceptions is that a person's sex chromosomes always "match" their other sex characteristics.

Puberty and Secondary Sex Characteristics

During puberty, people typically experience increased levels of estrogen and testosterone, or increased levels of one hormone or the other, in their bodies. Changes in hormones result in many different features: facial hair, breasts, hips, an Adam's apple, a lowered voice, and so on. These are all secondary sex characteristics. Society designates certain secondary sex characteristics female, such as breasts, and others as male, such as facial hair.

Most people with anatomy that society considers female experience puberty between the ages of 7 and 19. When they enter puberty, they will generally begin to experience a menstrual cycle, also known as a period. This process is essentially a person's body preparing for pregnancy. Most people who are assigned female are capable of becoming pregnant after puberty.

As a person enters the menstrual cycle, their reproductive system begins to produce egg cells called ova or oocytes. The average cycle occurs over 28 days and consists of three phases: follicular, ovulatory, and luteal. If these eggs are fertilized with sperm during the ovulation phase, the person may become pregnant. In the luteal phase, if they have not become pregnant, the lining of the uterus sheds and leaves the body.

During puberty, people with anatomy society considers female typically experience other physical changes as well. Their hips begin to widen and they develop breasts, which vary in size from person to person. Hair begins to grow in their armpits, on their legs, and in their pubic region. The Palo Alto Medical Foundation outlines some of these bodily changes in the following chart:

Puberty Event	Age at Which It Happens
Growth of breasts	8 - 13
Growth of pubic hair	8 - 14
Body growth	9 1/2 - 14 1/2
First period	10 - 16 1/2
Underarm hair	2 years after pubic hair shows up
Acne	Around the same time as underarm hair

People with anatomy society considers male typically experience different changes during puberty. The testicles grow bigger, followed by the penis. The scrotum darkens, grows, hangs down, and develops hair follicles. Pubic hair begins to grow on the scrotum and above the penis, and often spreads over time. Generally, a person with a penis becomes able to ejaculate about a year after their testicles begin to grow. At this point, they are capable of reproduction. Vocal changes generally occur during this time as well. Their voice will lower over time, and often crack during the process. The Palo Alto Medical Foundation outlines some of these developments in the following chart:

Puberty Event	Age at Which It Happens
Growth of testicles & scrotal sac	10 - 13 1/2
Growth of pubic hair	10 - 15
Body growth	10 1/2 - 16 1/2
Growth of penis	11 - 14 1/2
Change in voice	About the same time as penis growth
Facial & underarm hair	About 2 years after pubic hair appears
Acne	About the same time as underarm hair appears

While these are the typical changes during puberty, everyone develops at their own rate and there are many variances in these developments. Often, people will experience changes that society does not typically associate with their assigned sex. For example, many people who are assigned male will also experience some level of breast development. The American Academy of Pediatrics (AAP) stated, "Early in puberty, most boys experience soreness or tenderness around their nipples. Three in four, if not more, will actually have some breast growth, the result of a biochemical reaction that converts some of their testosterone to the female sex hormone, estrogen."[1] Rather than following a strict binary, primary and secondary sex characteristics have a wide variety of possibilities.

Intersex Traits and Conditions

Many people have anatomy that is not "female" or "male." Variation can occur in any or all of a person's primary and secondary sex characteristics. For example, it is possible for a person to have "female" XX chromosomes and a penis, which is considered "male" genitalia. Vice versa, a person may have "male" XY chromosomes and a vagina, which is the "female" genitalia. There are a wide variety of these conditions, and they are all referred to under the umbrella term "intersex." Another current term for these conditions is DSD (disorders of sex development). Both of these terms can be controversial to different people, so it is important to ask individuals with these conditions how they identify.

Sometimes intersex traits are present at birth, while others do not become apparent until later in life, and still others are never discovered during a person's lifetime. This is one of the many reasons for the misconception that intersex traits are extremely rare. It is currently impossible to know exactly how many intersex infants are born, but estimates reveal these traits and conditions are much more common than most people realize. The American Psychological Association (APA) stated, "Some experts estimate that as many as 1 in 1,500 babies is born with genitalia that cannot easily be classified as male or female."[2] The United Nations' Human Rights division stated, "According to experts, between 0.05% and 1.7% of the population is born with intersex traits—the upper estimate is similar to the number of red-haired people."[3]

Sex Is a Spectrum

The concept of sex as a binary of "female" and "male" is scientifically inaccurate. A more realistic model is thinking of sex as a spectrum, or a continuum, with "female" sex characteristics at one end and "male" sex characteristics at the other. The Intersex Society of North America (ISNA) explained, "Intersex is a socially constructed category that reflects real biological variation … So nature doesn't decide where the category of 'male' ends and the category of 'intersex' begins, or where the category of 'intersex' ends and the category of 'female' begins. Humans decide."[4]

Peer sex educator Laci Green brings up another crucial point, saying that "it's important to remember the sex categories of male and female are actually generalizations, and those generalizations are created by us, by humans."[5] There is an incredible amount of variation even among "female" and "male" traits in size, shape, coloration, development, sensitivity, and many other factors. Intersex traits and conditions are normal variations of human anatomy. Claudia Astorino, an intersex activist, wrote, "Our [intersex] bodies are natural and normal and healthy; while some health problems are associated with some forms of intersex, simply being intersex isn't a health problem in and of itself."[6]

Intersex Individuals Talk About the Issues

In a 2015 BuzzFeed video, "What It's Like to be Intersex," four intersex young adults talked about their experiences with the hope of raising awareness of intersex conditions and offering support to intersex individuals. No two intersex people are biologically the same, and their personal stories are equally unique. These interviews are not meant to represent a universal intersex experience—there is no such thing. Rather, Pidgeon Pagonis, Emily Quinn, Alice Alvarez, and Saifa Wall opened up about their own individual lives to shed light on some of the issues many intersex people face.

The medical community often wrongly treats intersex traits as abnormalities that need to be "corrected." Even when intersex infants are perfectly healthy, doctors will often perform genital surgery for no reason other than to assign them a sex. Pagonis, who identifies as a queer gender nonconforming intersex person, talked about doctors who wanted to perform genital surgery on them: "They [the doctors] didn't even come up with an excuse, basically, in terms of a health-related reason. They instead just said it was about the appearance."[7]

The practice of performing medically unnecessary genital surgery reveals the harmful effects of the gender binary. When doctors and parents decide to alter an infant's anatomy simply to give them a sex, the societal pressure to label everyone as either female or male outweighs the rights of the infant and the risks of the surgery. Alvarez, who has XY chromosomes and typically female genitalia, shared: "They [the doctors] did a surgery to remove my testes and told my parents to take me home and just raise me as a girl. I didn't find out about it myself until I was 12."[8] Many intersex people, like Alvarez, do not know their own medical history because their parents and doctors keep it from them. This practice is deeply troubling as it disrespects the rights of intersex individuals.

In some cases, doctors perform genital surgeries *without* the informed consent of the parents. Even when parents do give consent, this practice often negatively impacts intersex children later in life. Genital surgeries are often irreversible, and many intersex people are dissatisfied with the outcome of surgeries they were forced to undergo as infants or children. When Wall was 13, doctors removed his testes. Wall, who identifies as an intersex man, described living by his assigned female gender until he was 25: "I was put on hormonal treatment which consisted of estrogen and progesterone. I just wanted to belong. I wanted to fit in. I didn't want to be different. So, even though I knew something felt amiss, I conformed."[9]

Societal pressure to fit into the female and male binary creates a harmful taboo around intersex traits and conditions. Quinn shared, "My doctors always told me there was nobody else like me. And so it just perpetuates a vicious cycle of shame and stigma that we can't break out of."[10] In reality, there are many intersex people in the United States and around the world, but intersex people can easily feel isolated. Quinn explained, "It's difficult for intersex people to find each other because from an early age, we're told not to talk about our bodies."[11] Accepting intersex traits and conditions as normal, natural variations of human anatomy is crucial for reshaping society's ideas about sex.

Informed Consent

Consent is a person's agreement to participate in a situation or action. A person can only give consent when they are in their right state of mind, and they can revoke their consent at any time. Informed consent means that a person understands the effects of an action before they agree to it. Intersex advocacy groups around the world argue that performing genital surgeries that are not medically necessary on infants and children is unethical because of the lack of informed consent.

Infants and children are incapable of giving informed consent. Even parents who educate themselves on intersex traits and the potential outcomes of a surgery do not have the authority to give informed consent on behalf of their child. These surgeries violate the rights of intersex infants and children.

There are many steps parents can take to ensure their intersex children have healthy, happy lives. ISNA proposed healthy ways for parents to care for their intersex children:

> What we do advocate is providing parents of intersex newborns—and within a couple of years, intersex children themselves—honest and accurate information about intersex, psychological counseling by professionals who are not intersex-phobic, medical help for any real medical problems, and especially referrals to other people dealing with the same issues.[12]

Pagonis attested to the importance of community. They say that "meeting other intersex people and finding a community or a support group can be one of the most important aspects in your healing process."[13] Intersex advocacy groups around the world help intersex people connect with others who can relate to their experiences. These organizations fight for the rights of intersex children and adults, work to increase public awareness of intersex people and the issues they face, and to destigmatize intersex traits and conditions.

Breaking the Binary

If sex is not a binary, why does society automatically divide people into female and male genders? Gender Spectrum explained that "Western culture has come to view gender as a binary concept, with two rigidly fixed options: male or female, both grounded in a person's physical anatomy."[14] Society's fundamental misunderstanding of sex shapes its ideas about gender. Traditionally, society has linked its concept of female anatomy to a female gender and its concept of male anatomy to a male gender. In reality, sex and gender are two different things. A person's assigned sex does not determine their gender. Adrian Ballou explained, "Our society has imposed gendered traits onto certain body parts and secondary sex characteristics. They actually are meaningless for determining that person's a/gender identity."[15]

There are many variances in sex characteristics beyond what society considers female and male anatomy. Even if a person's anatomy determined their gender, there would still be many genders beyond female and male. Society has created an artificial link between sex and gender that makes it difficult for people to express themselves freely, especially if their gender does not match the sex they were assigned at birth.

CHAPTER 2

What Is Gender?

Gender is many different things all at once, which makes it impossible to capture in one universal definition. People experience gender in both public and personal ways. While gender is part of who a person is as an individual, it also has a broader role in society. As people grow up, they are bombarded with messages about gender from family, friends, and the larger community. Before looking at the personal aspects of gender, it is important to first understand how gender works in society.

Gender Is a Social Construct

Society has historically believed that a person's sex determines many aspects of who they are, such as their appearance, abilities, interests, and behaviors. These aspects are all lumped under the term "gender." As society divides sex into a female and male binary, it also divides gender into a female and male binary, known as the gender binary.

Society determines which behaviors, occupations, skills, interests, and personality traits are "normal" for the female sex and which are "normal" for the male sex. Social norms based on a person's assigned sex are called gender roles. Gender roles are not universal—each society has its own variation of gender roles, and some cultures recognize more than two genders. A trait that is "masculine" in one culture may be considered "feminine" in another, and vice versa. These variations demonstrate that gender roles are a social construct, or "an idea that has been created and accepted by the people in a society."[16]

In the simplest of terms, ideas about gender are made up. A person is not born believing that pink is for girls and blue is for boys, that girls are passive and boys are bold, that women are instinctively compassionate and men are logical by nature, or any of the innumerable stereotypes about what is "feminine" and what is "masculine." Instead, these stereotypes are learned from external sources as a person grows up. The actions and attitudes of family, friends, teachers, classmates, and all acquaintances are absorbed. These interactions slowly shape a person's understanding of gender as one grows up, generally without them even noticing. Gender is also learned about through other sources: the news, religion, movies, television, music, books, magazines, advertisements, and many others. When similar messages are observed from multiple sources, a person begins to believe that these messages about gender must be true. This makes it easy to fall into the belief that these "differences" between the female sex and the male sex are natural, instinctual, or even biological.

THE HARMFUL EFFECTS OF GENDER ROLES

"Gender roles shape individual behavior not only by dictating how people of each gender should behave, but also by giving rise to penalties for people who don't conform to the norms ... This threat of punishment for stepping outside of gender norms is especially true for those who do not identify as male or female. Transgender, genderqueer, and other gender-nonconforming people face discrimination, oppression, and violence for not adhering to society's traditional gender roles." –Boundless Psychology

"Gender and Sociology," Boundless Psychology, May 26, 2016. www.boundless.com/psychology/textbooks/boundless-psychology-textbook/gender-and-sexuality-15/gender-414/gender-and-sociology-296-12831/

Gender roles are more complex—and more harmful—than a clean division between female and male. Society often sees the categories of "female" and "male" as competing forces. Rather than treating both women and men equally, men have historically had more social and economic power than women, and in many ways, this continues to be true today. Women have historically been discriminated against based on their sex. This type of discrimination is called sexism. While anyone can experience sexism, men have historically benefited socially and economically by discriminating against women and transgender people. Although there has been significant progress, sexism and violence toward women and transgender people is still abundantly evident today.

Even in the modern day, society still pressures women to meet many expectations of motherhood, housekeeping, and other traditionally feminine gender roles.

Gender is not the only basis for discrimination that women experience. Race, ability, religion, and many other factors can also impact the sexism and violence many women experience. Racial, religious, ableist, and other prejudices must be acknowledged and combated alongside sexism. Objectification, violence, and discrimination—especially at work—are just some of the issues women face.

Objectification

In both personal relationships and in the media, such as advertisements, women are often treated as sexual objects or possessions rather than as people. This behavior values women based on their physical appearance and holds women to unrealistic beauty standards that can lead to lowered self-esteem. Treating women this way is both disrespectful and dehumanizing. This objectification leads to further discrimination and violence against women.

Sexual and Physical Violence

Sexual and physical violence against women and abusive behaviors such as stalking continue to be a problem in society. The graph on the following page represents the impact of gender and race on a person's likelihood of being a victim of rape, violence, or stalking in their lifetime.

Rape, Violence, or Stalking Experienced in a Lifetime		
Women		Men
4 in 10	Native American or Alaska Native	4 in 10
4 in 10	Black	3.5 in 10
3.5 in 10	White	2.5 in 10
4 in 10	Latinx	3 in 10
5 in 10	Multiracial	4 in 10
2 in 10	Asian or Pacific Islander	N/A

These statistics represent women with a household income of $50,000 or more. Women with lower incomes are at even greater risk. This graph is adapted from a 2010 infographic developed by the Centers for Disease Control and Prevention.

Discrimination in the Workplace

Sexism against women exists within personal relationships and within social structures, such as work environments. One example is the wage gap between women and men. A 2015 study conducted by the Pew Research Center found that the wage gap between white men and women impacts women of color even more severely than white women.

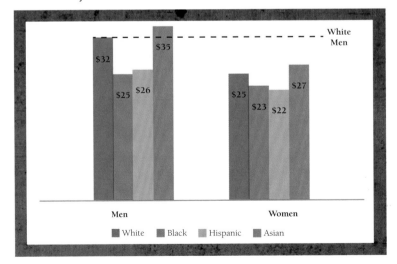

While white women experience sexism, black and Latina women experience a combination of sexism and racism. This information from the Pew Research Center shows how sexism and racism affect income.

Toxic Masculinity

Sexism and gender roles have a negative impact on everyone. People who are assigned male at birth face an immense amount of pressure from society—and often from their own family and friends—to fulfill unrealistic expectations of masculinity. Society glorifies hypermasculine traits, which creates a phenomenon that many people are currently calling "toxic masculinity." Writer Harris O'Malley explained:

> Toxic masculinity is a narrow and repressive description of manhood, designating manhood as defined by violence, sex, status and aggression. It's the cultural ideal of manliness, where strength is everything while emotions are a weakness; where sex and brutality are yardsticks by which men are measured, while supposedly "feminine" traits— which can range from emotional vulnerability to simply not being hypersexual—are the means by which your status as "man" can be taken away.[1]

1. Harris O'Malley, "The Difference Between Toxic Masculinity and Being A Man," The Good Men Project, June 27, 2016. goodmenproject.com/featured-content/the-difference-between-toxic-masculinity-and-being-a-man-dg/.

Gender in Childhood

Children absorb messages about gender at a rapid pace. Around age two, most children can distinguish the physical difference between typical female and male anatomy. By three years old, they can identify their own assigned sex. They also already understand which clothes, toys, and activities are "normal" for their assigned sex, and which are "off-limits." Children quickly learn which of their behaviors and preferences are praised, rewarded, or encouraged because of their assigned sex and which are rejected, mocked, or discouraged. Before a child has celebrated their fifth birthday, they are already beginning to internalize society's messages about gender.

Family and friends often give children toys based on gender roles. Children assigned as girls receive dolls, houses, stuffed animals, and other "feminine" toys, while children assigned

Many toys are rooted in stereotypes of how girls and boys should behave. Toys such as dolls and kitchen sets encourage girls to "play house," while toys such as guns and other weapons encourage boys to be aggressive.

as boys receive "masculine" toys such as cars, weapons, and sporting equipment. This separation of genders through toys is reinforced through the media children consume. Commercials show girls playing with dollhouses and boys playing with vehicles and action figures. Toys are physically separated into boys' and girls' aisles in most stores, and this division is generally marked by color: pink toys for girls and blue, green, red, and orange for boys. All of these factors send children (and adults) the message that boys and girls *naturally* like different things. In reality, children are often naturally attracted to toys, clothes, hobbies, and other activities outside of their imaginary gender boxes. However, all of these cultural influences, from family to television to toy aisles, push children to play with the toys that are associated with their assigned sex.

Even the language used to describe children often reinforces these gender roles. Children who are assigned as girls who enjoy "masculine" toys and activities are often called "tomboys," emphasizing their masculinity, while those who prefer "feminine" toys and activities are often called "girly girls." Children who are assigned as boys who prefer "feminine" things are often mocked and discouraged, while those who prefer "masculine" things are praised for fulfilling male expectations. These social effects create a lot of pressure to conform to gender roles, which can make it difficult for children to just be themselves. This is especially true for intersex and transgender children.

Gender Is an Identity

Gender is an important part of a person's individuality. It is one of the many qualities that help a person know who they are.

Gender can shape the way individuals see themselves, how they express themselves, and how they want others to see them. A person's internal sense of gender is their gender identity.

The relationship between social constructs and gender identities is complicated. Gender roles are social constructs, but a person's gender identity is personal and meaningful. According to writer Wiley Reading, "Gender identity is internal, deeply-rooted, and a central part of many people's senses of self."[17] Gender identity is deeper than society's messages and stereotypes about gender.

Most people have gender identities that match the sex and gender they were assigned at birth. This is described as "cisgender." Many people have gender identities that are not the same as the sex and gender they were assigned at birth. "Transgender" is an umbrella term that includes all people who have a gender identity that is different from the sex and gender they were assigned. However, not everyone who has a gender identity that differs from their assigned sex and gender identifies as transgender. Likewise, not everyone who identifies as transgender agrees with this definition. Some people consider transgender to be only a specific identity, not an umbrella term. It is important to respect each person's terms and definitions. For the purposes of this book, transgender will be used as an umbrella term.

The language used to describe gender identities evolves over time. Many terms that were once commonly used are now considered offensive. Even some of the terms that are common today may be considered outdated or offensive in the future. This section will look at some of the terms that many people currently use to describe their gender identities and the common definitions that accompany these terms. As gender identity is extremely personal, these terms can mean different things to different people. People need to respect the language individuals choose for themselves, while also understanding that a term might be meaningful to one person and offensive to another. Under no circumstances should a person label someone else with a gender identity. These terms should not be viewed as universal definitions that work for every person.

Transgender or Trans

In addition to acting as an umbrella term, the word "transgender" can also be a specific identity. Many people identify as transgender women or transgender men. The National Center for Transgender Equality (NCTE) offers the following definitions:

> *Transgender: A term for people whose gender identity, expression or behavior is different from those typically associated with their assigned sex at birth. Transgender is a broad term and is good for non-transgender people to use. "Trans" is shorthand for "transgender." (Note: Transgender is correctly used as an adjective, not a noun, thus "transgender people" is appropriate but "transgenders" is often viewed as disrespectful.)*

> *Transgender Man: A term for a transgender individual who currently identifies as a man.*

> *Transgender Woman: A term for a transgender individual who currently identifies as a woman.*[18]

Some transgender women sometimes refer to themselves as MTF, or "male-to-female," while some transgender men refer to themselves as FTM, or "female-to-male." This shorthand can be helpful for talking about issues specific to transitioning from living as a female to living as a male, and vice versa. Not all transgender women and men use these terms, and many people see transitioning as more complex than these phrases.

Nonbinary

The term "nonbinary" can also work in a number of different ways. Trans Student Educational Resources explained that nonbinary is a "preferred umbrella term for all genders other than female/male or woman/man … Not all nonbinary people identify as trans and not all trans people identify as nonbinary."[19] Not all people who identify as nonbinary also identify under the umbrella of transgender, and vice versa. It is completely up to each person to choose which language feels right for them.

Genderqueer

The word "queer" has a history of derogatory use, but many people are reclaiming the term in different ways. The Gay and Lesbian Alliance Against Defamation (GLAAD), an organization dedicated to LGBTQIA representation in the news and media, explained that genderqueer is a term "used by some people who experience their gender identity and/or gender expression as falling outside the categories of man and woman. They may define their gender as falling somewhere in between man and woman, or they may define it as wholly different from these terms."[20] While some definitions of genderqueer may sound very similar to some definitions of nonbinary, these words should not be used interchangeably, unless an individual identifies with both terms.

Jacob Tobia (pictured here) is an outspoken genderqueer advocate.

Gender Fluid

Some people do not feel as though their gender is one unchanging thing. Many who feel this way use the term "gender fluid" to describe their identity. In other cases, gender fluid can be a description of a behavior. As with all of these terms, it depends on the individual. The organization Gender Diversity stated:

> Gender fluidity conveys a wider, more flexible range of gender expression, with interests and behaviors that may even change from day to day. Gender fluid people do not feel confined by restrictive boundaries of stereotypical expectations of women and men. For some people, gender fluidity extends beyond behavior and interests, and actually serves to specifically define their gender identity. In other words, a person may feel they are more female on some days and more male on others, or

Ruby Rose is famous for her role as Stella Carlin in Orange Is the New Black.

possibly feel that neither term describes them accurately. Their identity is seen as being gender fluid.[21]

Not everyone who identifies as gender fluid interprets this term the same way. For example, a gender fluid person might not define themselves in terms of "feminine" or "masculine." Actor Ruby Rose describes her gender fluidity as follows:

Gender fluidity is not really feeling like you're at one end of the spectrum or the other. For the most part, I definitely don't identify as any gender. I'm not a guy; I don't really feel like a woman, but obviously I was born one. So, I'm somewhere in the middle, which—in my perfect imagination—is like having the best of both sexes.[22]

Bigender

Some people identify as two genders, such as female and male. Bigender people experience and express their identities in many different ways. Writer Jayson Flores explained, "Bigender people may feel male one day and female the next. The identification is different for each person as some may live for years with one gender and suddenly switch to the other. Everyone can do it their own way."[23] In Flores's case, "I identify mentally, spiritually, and emotionally as female, and only physically as a male. My gender expression, which is different from gender itself, is feminine in both cases."[24]

Genderless and Gender Neutral

Some people do not identify as feminine, masculine, or any gender, and instead see their gender identity as neutral. Other people are "genderless" and do not have a gender identity at all. In addition to genderless and gender neutral, "agender" and "neutrois" are two of the most common terms people identify with.

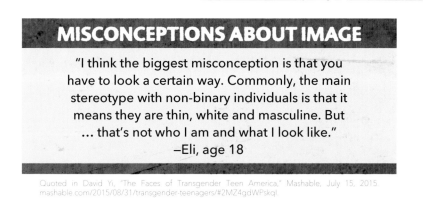

MISCONCEPTIONS ABOUT IMAGE

"I think the biggest misconception is that you have to look a certain way. Commonly, the main stereotype with non-binary individuals is that it means they are thin, white and masculine. But … that's not who I am and what I look like."
—Eli, age 18

Quoted in David Yi, "The Faces of Transgender Teen America," Mashable, July 15, 2015. mashable.com/2015/08/31/transgender-teenagers/#2MZ4qdWPskql.

Agender is another term that can be an umbrella term or a specific identity by itself. Trans Student Educational Resources explained that people who identify as agender "commonly do not have a gender and/or have a gender that they describe as neutral."[25] People who identify as agender might not identify under terms such as transgender, nonbinary, genderqueer, or gender nonconforming. To some, these terms imply identifying with a gender which does not match how they feel about their own lack of gender. Others might be comfortable with one or more of such terms—it all depends on the individual and there is no "right" or "wrong" way to identify as agender.

Definitions of neutrois are often very similar to definitions of agender, but the terms should not be used interchangeably. Neutrois.com explained, "Some neutrois [people] do feel completely genderless—that is, they have no gender, an absence of gender, or are null gendered. Others have an internal gender that is neither male, nor female, just neutral."[26] People who identify as neutrois may also identify as agender, nonbinary, or one or more other terms. Others may only identify as neutrois.

Cisgender Privilege

Cisgender people experience privilege because society has been designed for them. Countless aspects of daily life are divided into female and male categories: bathrooms, locker rooms, sports teams, clothing departments, hygiene products, organizations such as Girl Scouts and Boy Scouts, legal documents, and more. Cisgender people have a much easier time navigating these gender divides because no one questions their rights or choices. A cisgender girl can sign up for the girls' lacrosse team at her school without any trouble. A cisgender man can use the men's bathroom at work without worry. These seemingly small actions add up to an enormous amount of privilege that cisgender people can easily take for granted.

In other words, society considers being cisgender the "norm." Dr. K. J. Rawson explained, "It's an incredible and invisible power to not *need* to name yourself because the norms have already done that for you. You don't *need* to come out as heterosexual or cisgender because it is already expected."[27] Meanwhile, the transgender community has to fight for the same basic rights that cisgender people use without worry every day.

Cisgender privilege does not mean that cisgender people never face discrimination or difficulty. It simply means that they have an advantage in certain areas that the transgender community does not. Everyone's experiences are unique, and because there are many aspects to identity, every person experiences different combinations of privilege and difficulty. Sam Dylan Finch explained:

> For example, while it is true that I am transgender and experience disadvantages as a result, I am also a white person. So while I do experience struggles as a transgender person, my whiteness affords me racial privilege.
>
> It's also true that a transgender person of color, impacted by both racism and transphobia, will have a distinctly different experience of their oppression.[28]

A cisgender person does not have to feel bad about the areas in which they experience privilege, but they should look for ways to use that privilege to help others. Finch wrote, "Self-blame and self-hatred is not actually what checking our privilege is about ... Instead, think about privilege as an opportunity to build on your compassion and understanding. See it as an opportunity to be empowered to make a difference, however small it might be."[29]

Examples of Cisgender Privilege

These are just some of the many forms of privilege a cisgender person is likely to experience:

- They can use the bathroom and locker room that matches their gender identity without fear or harassment.

- They can participate in the gender-specific clubs, sports, and activities of the gender they identify with without facing discrimination.

- Their name and pronouns are always respected.

- People do not ask them invasive questions about their body.

- They do not have to fear that their gender identity will be "outed" to their family, friends, or community.

- They do not struggle to find work because of their gender identity, and they are less likely to be fired from their job because of their gender identity.

- They are less likely to experience homelessness than their transgender friends.

- They are less likely to experience police brutality than their transgender friends.

- They are less likely to experience a hate crime based on their gender identity.

- If they are the victims of a crime, there are no laws (such as "trans panic") that will make it easier for the criminal to escape charges.

Being an Ally to the Transgender Community

By admitting their privileges, a person can become a better ally to those who are being discriminated against. This is true for cisgender people who want to be better allies to the transgender community. Trans Student Educational Resources defined an ally as "Someone who advocates and supports a community other than their own," and explained that "Allies are not part of the communities they help."[30]

It is extremely important for cisgender people to step up and act as allies for the transgender community. They can use their positions of cisgender privilege to speak and act on behalf of the transgender community, which often struggles to have its concerns heard. Here are some important steps cisgender people can take to become better allies:

- Listen to transgender voices.
- Be educated. Listening is incredibly important, but it is not a transgender person's job to educate the cisgender people in their life. Chelsea Yarborough of the website Feminist Campus explained: "It's pretty exhausting to have to explain the nature of your oppression when you experience it every day. Do not rely on trans folks to educate you!"[31] Reading up on transgender resources, such as Trans Student Educational Resources or Gender Spectrum, can be a great place to start.
- Call out transphobia. Transphobia is intense dislike or hate toward transgender individuals, and it leads to discrimination against the transgender community. Even seemingly harmless actions can be deeply transphobic and damaging. Writer JR Thorpe said, "Words can be violent; there are many phrases that can be seriously hurtful to trans people. Educate yourself."[32] Part of a person calling out transphobia is acknowledging their own transphobic mistakes. If an offensive term is used, an inappropriate question is asked, or they acted in a transphobic way, it is important for them to admit their error and apologize.
- Use cisgender privilege to make spaces safe. Unfortunately, there are many environments where transgender people are not able to feel comfortable or, in some cases, physically safe. Cisgender people need to use their privilege to make environments safe and accepting in order for society to change for the better. Yarborourgh wrote:

As a cis person, your gender permits you entry into conversations and spaces that may not be safe for trans folks. Incorporate gender pronouns into your introductions in classes, club meetings, and everyday conversation. If you're planning an event, find a way to make gendered spaces such as bathrooms gender neutral, and make sure everyone knows where already existing gender neutral bathrooms are. Ask folks what their access needs may be before you call a meeting or plan an event to reduce any trouble folks may have in navigating the spaces you're wanting them to come to. Make it known that if people don't feel safe going into a gendered space like a bathroom, they can ask someone in the meeting to accompany them.[33]

Cisgender people should be careful not to single out transgender peers in their efforts to make spaces safer. It is also important for cisgender people to remember not to make assumptions about the needs of their transgender peers.

Gender Theory: Ways of Understanding Gender

If the gender binary is a social construct, but gender identity is a real and personal experience, then what exactly is gender? Even within the transgender community there are many different theories or ways of thinking about gender. Currently, one of the most dominant views is that gender is a spectrum.

Many people visualize the gender spectrum as a line with femininity at one end and masculinity at the other. Along this spectrum, there are many different gender identities ranging from extremely feminine, to genderless or neutral, to extremely masculine.

In this type of spectrum, gender identities are arranged by how feminine or masculine a person feels. Gender identities that are neither feminine nor masculine, and people who do not feel they have a gender identity, are placed in the middle.

Others visualize the spectrum as a Venn diagram. In this version of the model, characteristics that overlap multiple identities are represented in the overlapping of circles. For example, someone who identifies as both masculine and gender fluid is represented in the overlap between the "masculine" and "gender fluid" circles.

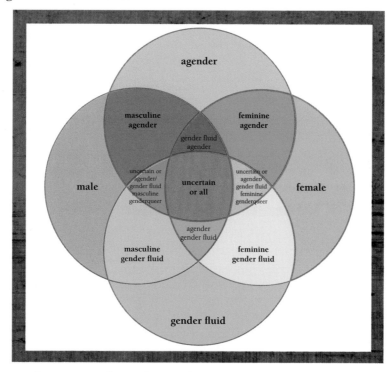

This user-created Venn diagram, featured on the social networking site Tumblr, is one way of viewing the gender spectrum. This model works for some people, but others do not identify with these categories.

These are just two examples of visualizing gender as a spectrum. While these visual tools can be helpful, it is important to realize that gender is much more complex and fluid than any diagram can represent. Thinking of gender as a spectrum works for many people, but it can also be problematic for others.

There are many other metaphors and visual tools for thinking about gender. For example, Wiley Reading has a different model of gender:

We tend to think of ... gender as a fixed quality, but really it's more of a constellation of traits.

Each man has a constellation of gender characteristics that together add up to "man."

Trans people also have gender constellations—a whole cloud of characteristics related to their gender.

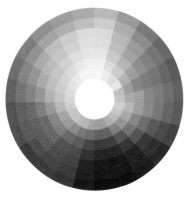

Thinking of gender as a range of colors, or as a color wheel, eliminates the "feminine" and "masculine" measuring system.

The ratios of traditionally masculine to traditionally feminine qualities may be different than you're used to, but that does not make a trans person's gender any less real or valid.[34]

Rather than a scale of femininity and masculinity, Reading sees each person's gender identity as a unique constellation of traits. This model helps show that gender is deeply personal and different for each person.

Others may prefer to visualize gender without the "female" and "male" binary in mind at all. For example, writer Adrian Ballou described gender as a range of colors:

Many people like to say that the binary gender system only allows us two colors, when really the full possibilities of gender exist as a whole range of color.

This analogy is more useful than "spectrum" because it allows for all genders to be measured not by the amount at which they "measure up" to the two most common gender identities and expressions, but simply by the way they just are.[35]

Ballou's view of gender does not describe identities in terms of how "feminine" or "masculine" they are. This model might be helpful for people who want to get away from thinking of gender as a binary.

CHAPTER 3

Navigating Gender Identity

It can be difficult for transgender people to navigate society's messages of what is "feminine" and what is "masculine" as they try to find what feels right for them. Many people demonstrate their gender identities through the clothing they wear, how they cut or style their hair, body language, and other physical aspects of themselves. The many ways gender identity shapes how a person presents themselves to the world is called gender expression. Like any other form of personal expression, gender expression is unique to each person. Gender can be expressed in many different ways.

Gender Expression

Although an internal sense of gender often shapes how people present themselves, gender identity and gender expression are two different things. Wiley Reading explained:

> Gender expression is the way in which you express your gender.
>
> Sometimes these expressions go along with socially sanctioned ideas of what is appropriate. For example, we live in a society that deems dresses appropriate for women, but not for men. But sometimes they don't.
>
> You may identify as a woman and dress in a traditionally feminine way. You may identify as a woman and dress in a traditionally masculine way. The point is that the two aren't necessarily related.[36]

Society has developed many stereotypes about gender expression. It categorizes certain appearances, types of clothing, and behaviors as feminine and others as masculine. However, human beings are more complex than this, and nearly everyone has a combination of both stereo-typically feminine and masculine characteristics, behaviors, and interests. These are merely soci-etal labels that do not represent a person's gender identity. Reading stated, "The way that someone *expresses* their gender is not necessarily a clue as to how they *identify* their gender."[37]

Makeup, hairstyles, and clothing can be empowering tools for a person to create their own style that makes them feel comfortable and in tune with their gender identity.

When Does a Person Know Their Gender Identity?

Many children quickly gain a sense of their gender identity. The AAP stated: "By age four, most children have a stable sense of their gender identity. During this same time of life, children learn gender role behavior—that is, doing *'things that boys do'* or *'things that girls do.'*"[38] However, this is not the case for everyone. Young children may explore gender, but later in life identify as cisgender. According to the AAP, "There is not enough research to know if this change means the child has learned to hide his or her true self due to social pressures"[39] or if the gender noncon-forming behavior was a phase.

Some children do not go through a questioning or explor-atory process, but simply know they identify with a gender other than the one they have been assigned. Activist Jordan Geddes shared: "Ever since I could remember, I'd always felt I'm a guy. From the age of 2, I would tell people I'm a boy. I even came up with a boy version of my birth name, and I would tell people I'm that. It was just never a question in my head."[40] Other transgen-der children take time to realize their identity. Graphic designer Robyn Kanner said, "I was about 6 years old when I picked up that I'm trans. You know how kids describe what they want to be when they grow up, like a firefighter? When I was 6 years old, I said I wanted to be a woman when I grew up."[41]

The discovery of gender identity is often a process. It can take people years to fully understand how they identify. Luna LeFort described how she came to understand her gender identity:

> Before 12 or 13, gender wasn't really an issue. You didn't care who you played with. I ended up hanging out more with girls. By 14, I wasn't interested in sports or associating with any of the masculine things at all. Around 16, I started Googling and found transgenderism. It was a realization: This makes sense. I was looking for my proper seat and I eventually found it. I was looking to be comfortable.[42]

Many people begin to explore or discover their gender identities as teenagers. Puberty can sometimes influence how a person feels about their gender. Lana Tong didn't question her gender identity until she was a teenager: "Around 16, when I hit male puberty, I thought: 'No. This is the wrong one.' I wanted to go through that *other* one." Tong began to hormonally transition to and present as female in her later teen years. When she was interviewed at 18, Tong said, "There's male, female and I don't fit into either of those. What I feel right now is a-gender."[43]

Not everyone who is transgender realizes their gender identity in childhood or even as a teenager. Emily Prince, a lawyer and a blogger, said, "There were varying points in time when I knew something was different about me. I didn't put all the pieces together in a way that I was ready to declare to anyone until after law school, when I was 22."[44] Still other people see discovering their gender identity as a process that began in childhood. Filmmaker and activist Kortney Ziegler said, "I accepted that being trans is part of my life's journey around 24 years old. It was a long-term realization, from birth to the moment I decided to live socially as a male."[45]

There is no time frame on discovering gender identity. Some people do not fully realize their gender identity until they are well into adulthood. Others describe their gender identity as something they were born understanding. For many people, gender is a fluid experience that changes throughout the course of their lifetime. No matter how young or how old a person is, their identity is valid and deserves respect.

Gender in Different Cultures: Two Spirit

As gender is a social construct, cultures around the world all have their own unique variations of gender roles. Unlike the West, some societies recognize more than two genders. These gender identities are rooted in specific cultures' concepts of gender, and should only be used to describe the gender of people within that culture.

Many Native American cultures have a concept of a gender identity now called Two Spirit. NativeOUT explained, "A Two Spirit person is a male-bodied or female-bodied person with a masculine or feminine essence. Two Spirits can cross social gender roles, gender expression, and sexual orientation."[1] Definitions of Two Spirit may vary across communities or mean different things to individuals. This terminology and the identity itself are unique to Native American cultures, and therefore non-Native American people should not describe their own gender identities in this way. Non-Native Americans using the term Two Spirit is culturally appropriative because they are claiming authority to a deeply meaningful aspect of a culture they do not belong to.

1. "Two Spirit 101," NativeOUT, August 9, 2016. nativeout.com/twospirit-rc/two-spirit-101/.

Uncertainty and Feeling "Not Trans Enough"

Many people struggle with feeling uncertain about their gender identity, and this is perfectly normal. Sam Dylan Finch shared: "For a while … I felt like I needed to know exactly what I wanted, and I spent too much time agonizing over it. I wish I hadn't. I wish someone had given me permission to be confused, to be unsure, to be afraid."[46] A person may feel the need to "figure out" their gender identity. It is important to remember that gender can be a fluid experience. Experimenting, exploring, and even uncertainty are all normal parts of experiencing gender. Writer Mia Violet wrote, "You can try different labels for your gender. You don't have to denounce your gender and take up another one immediately; no one will brand it into your skin. You can experiment. It's okay to try on one identity and then later change your mind."[47]

Uncertainty can be difficult for transgender people because they may worry they are somehow "not trans enough" if they are not completely sure of their identity. Many transgender individuals share that they sometimes wonder things such as, "Am I really trans?" This sense of insecurity can come from society's lack of acceptance for transgender people. Finch explained:

> There's this culture of interrogation around transness—namely, that trans people have to prove that they're trans (to get respect, to get healthcare, to find support).

> We constantly have our validity called into question by cis and trans people alike. It leads us to internalize this voice of doubt and to intensely question ourselves as society at large does to us.[48]

Feelings of not being "trans enough" can come from a variety of places. Unfortunately, sometimes the idea that there are certain standards of trans-ness come from within the transgender community.

When one person's definition of transgender is very different from another person's, it can lead some people to question who is "trans enough." Mia Violet offered this advice on dealing with disagreements in the transgender community:

> It's okay to disagree with other trans people. As long as what you're saying isn't harming anyone else, it's okay to disagree with concepts and terms related to being trans. I know people, friends even, who will disagree with things I've said here, but that's the point. Your gender identity is a very intimately personal part of you, if you disagree with someone's perception of what being transgender means to you then that's fine.[49]

Coming Out

It can be extremely challenging for transgender people to share their gender identities with their family, friends, and community. Blatant discrimination against transgender people and society's strict enforcement of the gender binary create a hostile

Finding Words for a Nonbinary Identity

Sam Dylan Finch, who is nonbinary himself, offers suggestions on how to explain your nonbinary identity to others:

1. *What you are not: "A lot of people perceive me as…"*

2. *A word that describes what you are: "I've been trying out the word ___ to describe my gender."*

3. *Clarification on what that word means: "To me, this word means…"*

4. *Why this is important: Explain how being non-binary has made you feel, using the words "I have felt …" You could talk about how happy your non-binary identity makes you, or about how difficult it has been for you … or maybe both!*

For example, in my coming out, I explained it like this:

"Even though you may see me as a woman, on the inside, I am not a woman and I am not a man. I've been using the word 'genderqueer' to describe my gender, which means that I don't identify with either. If you placed me on a spectrum, with 'masculine' being at one end and 'feminine' being at the other, I'm somewhere in-between. Identifying as genderqueer has made me feel so much better because being seen as a woman made me feel so distressed and unhappy."[1]

1. Sam Dylan Finch, "8 Tips for Coming Out as Non-Binary," *Everyday Feminism*, July 29, 2015. everydayfeminism.com/2015/07/coming-out-as-non-binary/.

environment for transgender people. They may not feel physically or emotionally safe expressing their gender identity, or may choose to only share it with some people and not others. The process of a transgender person sharing their gender identity is commonly referred to as "coming out."

Many transgender people experience negative reactions when they come out at home, at school, at work, or in other areas of their lives. Others find acceptance from family and friends. Often, transgender people receive a range of positive and negative reactions from the different people they choose to come out to. In an interview with *Vox*, Katherine shared:

> *I used to have a horrible relationship with my mother. Since I started transitioning, it's been very positive, because she's seeing I'm happy now for the first time in my life. Because she's seeing the happiness in me, I guess we now have a closer bond.*
>
> *But I also have some uncles who refuse to acknowledge my existence now. One uncle refuses to talk to me at all ... I was really close to him before, but he cut off the relationship entirely because I'm trans. It still upsets me.*[50]

Finding acceptance from family and friends can be fulfilling and identity-affirming, while dealing with rejection or negative reactions, especially from loved ones, can be extraordinarily challenging.

Coming out is different for everyone, and there is no one perfect way or time to do it. However, it is always important that a transgender person feels physically and emotionally safe before they come out. Planning ahead can be crucial to ensure safety. Finch wrote, "Will your safety be at stake if you come out? If so, do you have a place that you can go? Could you lose your job? If so, are you familiar with the non-discrimination ordinances in your city, and do they protect you?"[51] While these questions can be difficult to consider, there are resources to help transgender people find safe, healthy ways to come out.

Resources such as LGBTQIA organizations can help transgender people find a sense of community and build accepting relationships.

Transgender, nonbinary, and gender nonconforming people may find it easier to come out to one or a few people they trust and are close to first.

This can be an extremely helpful step to take before coming out. Advocates for Youth recommended:

If you decide to share your identity, first tell people with whom you are comfortable and that you feel will understand. They might include a trusted teacher, counselor, sister, brother, parent, friend, or people at a youth group for gay, lesbian, bisexual, and transgender (GLBT) people.[52]

If someone shares their gender identity with another person, it is extremely important not to "out" them, or share their gender identity without their consent. It is possible that the person's physical and emotional well-being are at stake. GLAAD stated:

Knowing a transgender person's status is personal information and it is up to them to share it. Do not casually share this information, or "gossip" about a person you know or think is transgender. Not only is this an invasion of privacy, it also can have negative consequences in a world that is very intolerant of gender difference—transgender people can lose jobs, housing, friends, or even their lives upon revelation of their transgender status.[53]

As some transgender people are only out to certain people, they may present themselves differently in different situations. For example, a teenage transgender girl might express femininity and go by "she" and "her" pronouns and a name she has chosen for herself around friends, but at home, express masculinity and go by "he" and "his" pronouns and her given name at home. Transgender teens with parents who are prejudiced against the transgender community may not feel safe coming out to their family. Their physical and emotional safety could be at risk if they are "outed" by someone else.

Coming out is generally an ongoing process. Transgender people will have to decide whether or not to come out to the people already in their life, and then again with each new relationship they form. The attitudes of loved ones can also change over time, for better or worse. For example, sometimes transgender people find their friends and family support one aspect of their gender identity, but react negatively to another. Jordan

TRANS TEENS DESERVE SUPPORT

"It's important for trans teens, especially those of color, to know that there are people out there who love us, care for us, and want to see us grow to our greatest potential. These people are in our schools, our communities, online—everywhere. You just have to reach out and find them. These people transformed my life and I know they can impact yours as well. The world is changing, people's minds are expanding, and you deserve to be alive to see it and to live out your full potential." –Ellie Gaustria, age 21

Quoted in Raymond Braun, "7 Seriously Inspiring Trans Teens Reveal How They Stay Confident Even When People Try to Knock Them Down," *Seventeen*, December 30, 2015. www.seventeen.com/life/g2679/self-confidence-tips-transgender-teens/?slide=4.

Geddes shared, "The only real time I've had any pushback from my family is when I started taking hormones. Before, it wasn't anything medical or surgical. I think the medical aspect made it harder for them to accept."[54]

While the difficulties of coming out should never be dismissed, coming out is not always a scary or negative experience. Lily Carollo, who was interviewed by *Vox*, said, "My mom has been amazingly supportive. She's been pretty enthusiastic about the whole thing. She still remembers the day and date I told her 'I want to be a girl' for the first time."[55] Coming out can help transgender people to feel able to express themselves fully and openly. It can help them form closer relationships with people who accept them as they are.

Finding the Right Language

L anguage is an enormous part of identity. Names distinguish one person from another and help form a sense of self. The words used to describe a person's gender identity help them express themselves to others. Pronouns help a person describe other people, and often they signify a person's gender. Pronouns are substitutes for nouns, and are frequently used in reference to people. Pronouns such as "I," "me," "my," "you," "your," "she," "her," "he," "his," "they," and "their" are used in nearly every conversation a person has. In the English language, some pronouns are gendered. Society considers "she" and "her" feminine and "he" and "his" masculine. These distinctions are part of the social construct of gender—they are made up. However, because society associates gender with these pronouns, when a person refers to other people using these pronouns, they are ascribing a gender to them whether they intend to or not.

The Importance of Pronouns

Many transgender people are not comfortable with the pronouns associated with their assigned sex, and instead identify with a different set of pronouns that they feel better suits their gender identity. These are often described as "preferred pronouns." While many transgender people are comfortable with this term, it is better to simply say "pronouns." In BuzzFeedYellow's "Why Pronouns Matter for Trans People" video, Ian Harvie explained, "It's not even preferred pronoun because it is their pronoun."[56] The word "preferred" makes it sound as though there are other acceptable options, but you are the only person who gets to decide your pronouns.

If a person is not comfortable with the pronouns associated with their assigned sex, finding pronouns that they feel good about can be an identity-affirming process. ReachOut, an online resource for teens, outlined important things for a person to keep in mind as they figure out the pronouns that work for them:

- *It's okay to switch pronouns as many times as you want. You might try out different pronouns for a while to see which ones fit you best. Be patient with yourself during this process, and don't get discouraged if it takes some time to find ones that fit.*

- *You might also find that there isn't an "endpoint" to your pronoun journey and that what works best for you is switching between pronouns or having people use a mix of pronoun sets.*

- *Gender trumps grammar. Language is evolving all the time. It's okay to use the singular "they" and newer pronouns. If you feel like none of the pronouns that have been created so far fit you, you can even make up your own![57]*

Activist Kat Blaque said, "If you care about someone, you'll respect who they are. And part of respecting trans and nonbinary people is using the right pronoun."[58] A person deserves to have their identity respected, and to be described with language they are comfortable with. Using the pronouns that a person is comfortable with shows them that their gender identity is respected, and also that they are respected as a person.

Gender-Neutral Pronouns

Anyone can choose to go by "she" and "her," or "he" and "his," or a combination of both, even if they do not identify as strictly female or male. However, many people are not satisfied with these two options because they each carry stereotypes and ideas that are rooted in the gender binary. Blaque explained, "There are some situations we really put way too much stock into whether or not somebody is a man or a woman. There's a lot of situations that we just don't need to necessarily have gendered language."[59] In other cases, people might identify with femininity and masculinity, but these polarized pronouns still do not feel right. Harvie said, "For a long time, a lot of people have felt that they don't fit into the mold of primarily he or primarily she, or maybe they feel they're a blend of both, and that there's not really a word for that."[60]

Gender-neutral pronouns are developing to fill these gaps in gender language. As of 2016, the most popular gender-neutral choice in English is the singular form of "they." This word describes an individual person without ascribing a gender. For example, "Robin always plays their bass after school. They're a very talented musician." In 2015, the American Dialect Association declared the singular form of "they" to be the Word of the Year. These words have become an empowering option for transgender, nonbinary, and gender nonconforming people who do not want to identify themselves with feminine or masculine words.

All About Respect

One of the most important steps in respecting someone's pronouns is to avoid making assumptions. Blaque said, "We're

Grammar Is Changeable

Grammar may seem like a code of unbreakable rules, but it is actually changing and growing with the culture all the time. Some of these happen so subtly that people do not even notice them, and many people who notice do not care as long as the meaning of a word or sentence is clear. For instance, in the past, the word "stream" was used to define a flow of liquid or gas. After technology advanced to the point where people could use the Internet in their homes, another meaning was added to the word stream: a flow of data.

These changes are important to note because people who use "they" instead of gendered pronouns may be corrected by people who dislike that they are breaking a grammar rule. In English, "they" is officially a plural pronoun, but English-speaking people have been using the word "they" as a singular pronoun for centuries—even famous writers such as Jane Austen, Geoffrey Chaucer, and William Shakespeare. Saying that a person cannot refer to themselves with the word "they" because it is not grammatically correct is not a valid argument.

used to looking at someone and assuming what their pronouns are. But assuming pronouns can impact trans and nonbinary people in a very negative way."[61] Making assumptions about a person's pronouns is the equivalent to making assumptions about that person's gender identity. Writer Joli St. Patrick wrote:

> When you misgender me, you tell me many things. You tell me that you know who I am better than I know myself. You tell me you are not safe or trustworthy. You tell me you have scrutinized my physical appearance, made invasive extrapolations, and sorted me without my consent into a category based on your conclusions.[62]

Assumptions about a stranger's gender identity are based on the stereotypes of femininity and masculinity resulting from the gender binary. When a person's gender identity is assumed, the gender binary and its narrow concepts about femininity and masculinity are being perpetuated. Spoken word artist Kit Yan said:

> By not assuming and respecting people's pronouns, you shift your view of the world to one that sees humans for the complicated folks that they are. You are saying 'I am asking how you see yourself,' because we are not entitled to know or guess people's identity.[63]

In short, instead of assuming what a person's pronouns are, they should be asked what their pronouns are.

Normalizing Pronouns as Part of Introductions

Conversations about pronouns can be awkward, especially when people are meeting for the first time. Writer Petey Gibson stated:

> If you're not sure the pronoun that someone uses, ask them. "Hey, what pronoun do you use?" It is a simple and direct way to find out, and then using that pronoun, even if it doesn't slip off the tongue easily at first, will become second nature in no time. And using the pronoun that that person uses can entirely change the impression they have of the place they hold in this world. What a simple gift to give somebody.[64]

When each person is being introduced, it can make the situation more comfortable for everyone to share their own pronouns.

In group settings, such as the first day of class, having everyone introduce themselves and their pronouns can

Talking about pronouns does not have to be awkward—initiating a conversation and asking someone's pronouns shows respect.

be a positive way to ensure everyone feels comfortable and safe. Writer West Anderson describes this as a "pronoun round." They wrote:

This practice takes the pressure off trans people to announce their pronouns to the rest of the group and makes asking for and sharing pronouns a normal part of introductions. If a space is made for everyone to share their pronouns before discussion begins, it can avoid misgendering a group member unknowingly or putting a trans person on the spot to announce their pronouns to a group alone. It works to create spaces in which we don't assume someone's pronouns from their appearance.[65]

Anderson explained, "The purpose of a pronoun round is to normalize the sharing of pronouns so that everyone can be correctly referred to without 'othering' trans people."[66] E-sports journalist Amanda Stevens also believes in the importance of "making pronouns a normal part of our introduction system." She explained, "Normalization is the same thing as inclusivity."[67] Stevens feels that when conversations about gender and pronouns are made the norm, a new, inherently inclusive "normal" can be created.

Misgendering Language

Misgendering, or referring to someone by a gender other than their gender identity, can take many forms. Any situation in which a person is labeled as a gender they do not identify as is an act of misgendering. Unfortunately, pronouns are one of the most common ways people are misgendered. This can happen in any setting—at school, at work, out in public, or even at home. In any situation, misgendering is harmful and unacceptable. Author

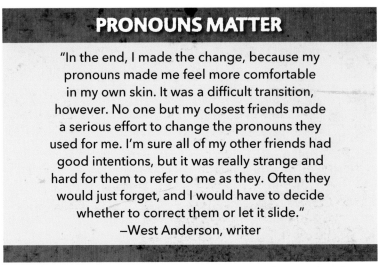

PRONOUNS MATTER

"In the end, I made the change, because my pronouns made me feel more comfortable in my own skin. It was a difficult transition, however. No one but my closest friends made a serious effort to change the pronouns they used for me. I'm sure all of my other friends had good intentions, but it was really strange and hard for them to refer to me as they. Often they would just forget, and I would have to decide whether to correct them or let it slide."
—West Anderson, writer

West Anderson, "Pronouns and Misgendering," *The Body Is Not An Apology*, December 2, 2014. thebodyisnotanapology.com/magazine/pronouns-and-misgendering/.

and performer Kate Bornstein explained, "Misgendering a person by using an incorrect pronoun is an act of disrespect."[68] In a *Vox* interview, Robyn Kanner shared: "It's like being kicked in the gut over and over. There was a while during my transition in which I tallied how often I was misgendered, and it topped off at 35 times."[69] Pronouns, names, and language are important tools for validating identity. No one has the right to use those tools in a way that makes someone uncomfortable.

Accidents do happen, and sometimes misgendering is an unintentional mistake. Anderson wrote, "If you mess up (which happens, I still do it too), apologize, correct the pronoun, and move on. That's all that's needed."[70] It is important to remember an apology is about the person who was wronged. The Lesbian, Gay, Bisexual, and Transgender Resource Center of the University of Milwaukee stated:

> A lot of the time it can be tempting to go on and on about how bad you feel that you messed up or how hard it is for you to get it right. But please, don't! It is inappropriate and makes the person who was mis-gendered feel awkward and responsible for comforting you, which is absolutely not their job.[71]

The Messages Misgendering Sends

Misgendering communicates disrespect in many ways. In his article, "What You're Actually Saying When You Ignore Someone's Gender Pronouns," writer and activist Sam Dylan Finch outlined some of the messages that misgendering someone can send:

1. *I know you better than you know yourself ...*

2. *I would rather hurt you repeatedly than change the way I speak about you ...*

3. *Your sense of safety is not important to me ...*

4. *Your identity isn't real and shouldn't be acknowledged ...*

5. *I want to teach everyone around me to disrespect you ...*

6. *Offending you is fine if it makes me feel more comfortable ...*

7. *I can hear you talking, but I'm not really listening ...*

8. *Being who you truly are is an inconvenience to me ...*

9. *I would prefer it if you stopped being honest with me ...*

10. *I am not an ally, a friend, or someone you can trust ...* [1]

1. Sam Dylan Finch, "What You're Actually Saying When You Ignore Someone's Gender Pronouns," Let's Queer Things Up!, September 15, 2014. letsqueerthingsup.com/2014/09/15/what-youre-actually-saying-when-you-ignore-someones-preferred-gender-pronouns/.

If a person is misgendered in any capacity, they have a right to be upset. They deserve to feel safe and respected.

Continual misgendering is very different from an accident. Anderson explained, "I want to be clear: The thing that hurts me most is not when someone messes up my pronouns. It's when they know my real ones, but they don't even try to correct themselves. They just let it sit there, and it's on me to bring it up, *again*, that 'It's *they*, not *she*.'"[72] When one person misgenders someone, their actions can lead to others misgendering the individual as well. Finch wrote:

> When you continue to use the incorrect pronouns, you are teaching everyone around you to use those same (incorrect) pronouns. Your transgender friend now has to correct not only you, but all of the people you've taught to use those same pronouns. You are working against them, and forcing them to come out as transgender over and over again. You are making their already very difficult job much, much harder.[73]

Choosing a New Name

Transgender people often choose a new name for themselves. They may choose a name that reflects their gender identity, or a gender-neutral name. Some people decide to legally change their

Eliminating Unnecessarily Gendered Language

Society is full of unnecessarily gendered language and phrases. Teachers address their classes as "boys and girls," waiters call their customers "sir" or "miss," friends call each other "bro," "man," or "dude." While this language seems harmless, it perpetuates the gender binary and erases transgender and nonbinary identities. It also creates a culture where people are easily misgendered. Adrian Ballou wrote that when a person uses gendered language, "You run the risk of misgendering someone, using sexism to justify your gender judgments, enacting sexism by interacting with someone based on their (a)gender identity, and generally being rude—because it's rude to assume that you know someone else better than they themselves do."[1] One alternative to gendered language when addressing a stranger is to simply tell them your name and ask for theirs. Saying, "Excuse me," to get someone's attention is another alternative to calling someone "sir" or "miss." These simple gestures can help transgender people feel comfortable and accepted.

1. Adrian Ballou, "7 Tired Phrases That Marginalize Trans People—And What to Use Instead," *Everyday Feminism*, February 3, 2015. everydayfeminism.com/2015/02/phrases-marginalize-trans-people/.

names, while others simply go by new names in their daily lives. Still others do not change their name at all. Colt Keo-Meier, a clinical psychologist who works with transgender patients and who is transgender himself, explained: "It helps [other] people to start seeing and thinking about you differently—even if your body hasn't changed, or if body changes aren't part of your transition plan, they still have to call you something different."[74] As with all experiences, choosing a new name—or choosing to keep a given name—is different for each person.

Choosing a new name can be an empowering part of embracing gender identity. Writer Fred McConnell shared how deciding to take a new name was part of accepting his own identity:

> *From a young age, I collected a list of names—all for boys, or at least gender-neutral. I said they'd be for my posse of sons. It started out on my mum's computer before being transferred to my phone and buried at the bottom of my notes app. When I decided that transition was right for me, I went back to this list. This is because when I had made peace with being trans, I also accepted that this list had, in part, actually been for me.*[75]

McConnell eventually chose first and middle names that were already a part of his family's history: Fred Reuben. He wrote, "Asking everyone to call me by a different name was a daunting part of my transition. But choosing one with ancestral links made the change easier for others and for me."[76]

For some people, asking for family members' opinions can be very meaningful. Rocco (who chose not to share a last name) said: "My parents were really supportive and great, so I asked them to be involved in the process with me. They named me after my great-grandfather. I liked the idea of having my parents name me again."[77] For others, a collaborative approach feels more natural. YouTuber Jamie Raines, whose videos are posted under the username Jammidodger, made a list of names he liked and went over it with friends and family. He explained, "Jamie kind of seemed to stand out as the favorite, so I kind of trialed it for a bit. It felt right, I really liked it, and, you know, people said it suited me so I stuck with it."[78]

Chaz Bono changed his name from Chastity to Chaz after he decided to transition from female to male.

Some people might not want to choose a family name, or even involve their family in the decision process at all. It all depends on the person, the relationships they have, and their unique situation. Sometimes, finding a brand new name without any associations feels right. Silas Hansen shared that "the thing I love most about the name Silas is that I don't know anyone else with that name. I've never met another Silas and so I don't have a picture in my head of what one looks like, sounds like, acts like. Silas is a blank slate."[79]

There is no right or wrong way for a person to find a name they love. Inspiration can come from anywhere. Greta Martela explained how she chose her name based on her old video game persona:

> For years before I transitioned I played computer role playing games with female characters. One game in particular, Icewind Dale, allowed me to create six female characters that would work together ... I knew that there was a name that I used in one of my many saved games that would be perfect for me. I eventually found the saved file and opened it up in a text editor to find the missing name. GRETA![80]

Finding a name with meaning, family history, or one that simply feels right can be a powerful experience.

Getting Comfortable with a New Name

Navigating a new name can be difficult, and this is completely normal. Sometimes people need to try out multiple names before they find the right one. Even when a person finds a new name they like, adjusting might still be challenging. Hansen shared how uncertain he felt the first time he was called by his chosen name:

> It felt so weird, so not normal *to be called Silas instead of Lindsay. I immediately regretted my decision. What if this meant I was wrong about being transgender and I never should have asked people to call me something else? What if I was right, but had chosen the wrong name? Was it too late to send another email, begging everyone to call me Andrew, or Charlie, or Sam? I hadn't expected it to be so hard— not for me at least, since I had wanted a new name—a male name— for so long, and since Silas felt so perfect in theory.* [81]

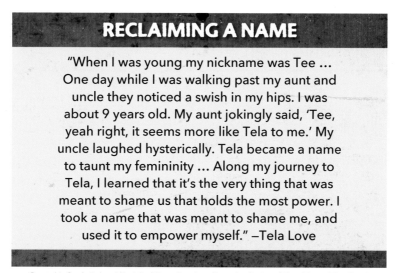

RECLAIMING A NAME

"When I was young my nickname was Tee ... One day while I was walking past my aunt and uncle they noticed a swish in my hips. I was about 9 years old. My aunt jokingly said, 'Tee, yeah right, it seems more like Tela to me.' My uncle laughed hysterically. Tela became a name to taunt my femininity ... Along my journey to Tela, I learned that it's the very thing that was meant to shame us that holds the most power. I took a name that was meant to shame me, and used it to empower myself." –Tela Love

Quoted in Sarah Karlan, "We Asked Trans People to Share the Stories of Their Names," BuzzFeed, March 1, 2016. www.buzzfeed.com/skarlan/we-asked-trans-people-to-share-the-unique-stories-behind-the?utm_term=.vnq5gqZqz7#.saGnm4O4zd.

Even though Hansen felt unsure at first, he kept the name Silas. He wrote, "I can carry that name with me as I learn how to be a man, learn to navigate this land of men's bathrooms and facial hair and talking to girls as a straight man without losing sight of who I am, who I used to be. And, in the end, what more could I want from a name?"[82] Although it can be hard to go through the process of changing a name, many people have found it be a liberating and fulfilling experience in the long run.

CHAPTER 5

Gender Expression and Transitioning

Many transgender people experience some form of gender dysphoria. The American Psychiatric Association explained:

> Gender dysphoria involves a conflict between a person's physical or assigned gender and the gender with which he/she/they identify. People with gender dysphoria may be very uncomfortable with the gender they were assigned, sometimes described as being uncomfortable with their body (particularly developments during puberty) or being uncomfortable with the expected roles of their assigned gender.[83]

Dysphoria can take many forms and it affects everyone differently. Some transgender people do not experience dysphoria at all. Writer Zinnia Jones stated, "Not all trans people have significant gender dysphoria or experience their dysphoria in the same way: different trans people may be uncomfortable with different aspects of their assigned sex, their body, their presentation, the gender role expected of them, and so on."[84]

Gender Dysphoria

Gender dysphoria used to be called "Gender Identity Disorder" by the APA. Referring to this experience as a "disorder" was deeply offensive to the transgender community because it implied there was something wrong or unnatural about being transgender. In 2013, the APA changed this term to "Gender Dysphoria" in its fifth edition of the *Diagnostic and Statistical Manual of Mental Disorders* (*DSM-5*). The APA acknowledged the need for a more respectful term and felt this change was an important step toward eliminating the stigma surrounding the transgender community. However, many still object to classifying dysphoria in the *DSM-5*. GLAAD explained:

The necessity of a psychiatric diagnosis remains controversial, as both psychiatric and medical authorities recommend individualized medical treatment through hormones and/or surgeries to treat gender dysphoria. Some transgender advocates believe the inclusion of Gender Dysphoria in the [DSM] is necessary in order to advocate for health insurance that covers the medically necessary treatment recommended for transgender people.[85]

Society often reduces the transgender experience to "being born in the wrong body." For many transgender people, this idea is stereotypical, inaccurate, or offensive. In a BuzzFeed article of artists illustrating their dysphoria, participant Felix explained, "'Being trapped in the wrong body' was never a phrase that really stuck with me because I think that sets my body in the wrong light. There are a lot of things my body does really well—it's just that it had the wrong set of building blocks when it was developing its look."[86] Dysphoria feels different for each person, and it should never be oversimplified or dismissed.

Certain sensations, events, or interactions can trigger feelings of dysphoria in a person. The causes of dysphoria are different for everyone. Some people experience dysphoria during particular tasks. Wiley Reading shared, "Showering is the most jarring part of my day."[87] Dysphoria can also be caused by external forces, such as family and friends. Amanda Stevens shared, "I didn't have any body dysphoria until people told me how not-a-woman I was."[88] She explained that many people tried to influence how she presented herself and pushed her to be more stereotypically feminine. This pressure to change herself caused her to begin experiencing dysphoria. Stevens said people in her life had the attitude of, "You're trying to be a girl, here are some things you can do to be a girl. Instead of saying, 'You're already a girl. You be you.'" Stevens explained that in her case, "I didn't have any of those insecurities until people presented them to me."[89]

Handling Gender Dysphoria

As dysphoria affects everyone differently, each person experiencing dysphoria will probably find their own ways of handling the symptoms. In any case, it is important to practice self-care. This

Describing Their Dysphoria

In 2016, BuzzFeed published an article titled, "We Asked People to Illustrate Their Gender Dysphoria." These are some of the descriptions the participants of this project shared about their experiences with dysphoria:

For me, my assigned gender has always been a box I was put into without my permission. It's restricting, and suffocating, and for most of my life it completely obscured who I was, like a cloud of pink that hides my inner colors from the world. It often feels like I'll never really be able to break out of the box, so instead I do my best to change its colors and make the box a place I can survive in. —Cael

To me, dysphoria comes mostly from people's gazes and words. They see me as a "girl" and call me as such—even in the most innocent way—simply because they don't know. Being called that,..because of my body shape, feels like being trapped into a tight envelope made out of "girl" stereotypes and expectations. A "girl suit" that is slowly choking me. The more they call me girl, the more the "girl suit" takes over, covering my real self, my real colors. —Pimeälex

My mind copes with dysphoria in strange ways. I am a transmasculine person, and I almost always feel disconnected from my body, like I don't have one or like I'm not even in my body. Because my brain doesn't seem to recognize my body as my own, I don't feel intense dysphoria about what seems "wrong" about it. —Anonymous[1]

1. Quoted in Sarah Karlan, "We Asked People to Illustrate Their Gender Dysphoria," BuzzFeed, May 10, 2016. www.buzzfeed.com/skarlan/we-asked-people-to-illustrate-what-their-gender-dysphoria-fe?utm_term=.yyp29MDMr3#.gfWb2DgDwB.

means they need to make their emotional and physical needs a priority, and give themselves permission to do things that make them feel good.

Finding ways to assert individual identity can help some people handle their dysphoria. Clothing, hairstyles, makeup, and other forms of gender expression can be empowering and helpful for alleviating dysphoria. Some people find body modifications help them feel more in control over their bodies as well. Writer Jenny Crofton explained, "Every time I get a tattoo or a piercing I feel more like my true self. Making alterations to my flesh empowers me to feel in command of my body, and capable of shaping it in ways that better express who I am."[90]

Embracing other aspects of one's identity can sometimes help with dysphoria, as well. Crofton explained how connecting with his culture helps him handle dysphoria:

More permanent alterations to one's appearance can help people feel like they are in control of their bodies and feel good in their own skin.

> As we develop our sense of gender, we shape ourselves in relation to our cultures. But oftentimes, people of color and others find themselves in a social context that does not represent the cultures that they identify with. This cultural estrangement can frustrate one's relationship with their gender and exacerbate feelings of dysphoria.

> I'm not just a man. I'm an Armenian man. In my quest for masculinity, I had been trying to define myself on Western terms, and it wasn't working. The frustration I experienced had an adverse effect on my dysphoria. I have since realized that I crave a sense of masculinity that is not reflected in the culture around me.[91]

Gender expression and roles are vastly different from culture to culture. Like Crofton, finding ways to connect with a cultural identity can sometimes help combat dysphoria.

Professional help from a psychologist, counselor, or therapist who is qualified to assist transgender patients may also be incredibly helpful to handling dysphoria and other difficulties a transgender person may face. It is important for transgender people seeking mental health treatment to find a professional who is accepting of the transgender community and who they personally feel comfortable talking to.

Ways of Altering Gender Expression

Dysphoria can take the form of someone wishing they had certain body parts, wishing they did not have certain body parts, or a combination of these feelings. Many people find that altering their body's appearance with nonmedical tools can help with gender dysphoria. Packing, tucking, padding, and binding are all common practices that allow people to take control over their appearance. Not everyone who alters their appearance suffers from dysphoria, and using these tools does not always mean that dysphoria will stop.

Packing is "having a non-flesh penis (sometimes referred to as a packer or a prosthetic penis). Some people view their non-flesh penis as a part of their body and don't consider themselves to be 'packing.' Many folks refer to this part just as their penis, rather than as a packer or prosthetic penis."[92] Packing can help people look and feel more masculine, which may help with dysphoria.

Tucking "refers to the practice of hiding the penis and testes so they are not visible in tight clothing."[93] Tucking can help create a more feminine appearance. Writer Meredith

Talusan stated, "There are a number of reasons why trans women tuck: both for our own sense of self, and to influence how others perceive us. For those of us who experience gender dysphoria related to the appearance of our bodies, it's a way for us to feel more like our bodies match the gender we feel inside."[94]

Padding, according to The Provincial Health Services Authority, is the "use of undergarments to create the appearance of larger breasts, hips, and buttocks." The organization adds, "Padding may help you feel more comfortable in your body. It may help you be read as your gender. It

Binders help create the appearance of a flat chest, which some people find extremely helpful for handling body dysphoria.

may also improve the way your clothing fits you."[95] Padding can help create a typically feminine figure.

   Binding "involves wearing tight clothing, bandages, or compression garments to flatten out your chest."[96] Reducing the appearance of breasts gives people a more masculine appearance and may help with dysphoria. Writer Meg Zulch stated,

Binder Safety

   Before a person practices any of these body-altering techniques, it is extremely important they research how to do so safely. It is especially important to research binding before they begin, as binding incorrectly can severely hurt their ribs, back, lungs, and skin. The following are things a person needs to consider every time they are binding:

- Never bind with Ace bandages or duct tape

- Never wear a binder that is too small

- Always take off a binder before going to sleep

- Never bind for more than eight hours at a time

- Take breaks from binding throughout the day

- Wash binders with soap and water regularly

- Always take off a binder before working out

   Even when they practice binding safely, it is important for them to evaluate their body's response every day. Writer Sarah Karlan suggested, "Check in with yourself each day after taking your binder off: How does your skin look and feel? Are you staying well-hydrated and stretching? It's important to note any changes that could be a sign that your binder is too tight or that you're wearing it for too long."[1]

1. Sarah Karlan, "All The Questions You Had About Chest Binding, But Were Afraid To Ask," BuzzFeed, March 17, 2015. www.buzzfeed.com/skarlan/all-the-questions-you-had-about-chest-binding-but-were-afrai?utm_term=.agPxm3g3kq#.hwlz0ErE8K.

"It's a silhouette that has the power to give many people, myself included, a boost of confidence, while bringing some of us a step closer to being our most authentic selves."[97] Wearing sports bras and several layers of clothing can be helpful alternatives to binding.

Transitioning

Transitioning is the process a transgender person undergoes when they begin to live by their gender identity instead of by the sex and gender they were assigned at birth. Choosing to transition, or not to transition, is a deeply personal process. GLAAD explained:

> Transition can include some or all of the following personal, medical, and legal steps: telling one's family, friends, and co-workers; using a different name and new pronouns; dressing differently; changing one's name and/or sex on legal documents; hormone therapy; and possibly (though not always) one or more types of surgery. The exact steps involved in transition vary from person to person.[98]

Some people choose to only transition socially. They may also only openly transition in certain areas of their life, or around certain people, where they feel safe and accepted. People who choose to medically transition have many options on how to do so. There is not one path to medically transitioning. Not all transgender people choose to transition either socially or medically; it is completely up to the individual.

Social Transitioning

Here are some of the steps a person may choose to take when socially transitioning:
- Taking a new name, either legally or informally.
- Using different pronouns.

Clothing that is considered "feminine" and "masculine" is part of the social construct of gender. Clothing can have whatever meaning the wearer chooses.

- Changing their gender expression through clothing, hairstyle, makeup or lack of makeup, and other aspects of their physical appearance.
- Coming out to family and friends.
- Coming out at school or at work. This often involves speaking with administration at school or Human Resources at work.
- Changing their gender marker on forms of identification, such as a driver's license or school I.D. The steps of this process depend on the state they live in and can be extremely difficult.
- Using bathrooms in school, at work, or in public that suit their gender identity.
- Participating in clubs, organizations, and activities that suit their gender identity. For example, joining the women's soccer team at their school or singing in a men's choir.
- Moving to a college dorm that suits their gender identity (if their college separates dorms by gender).

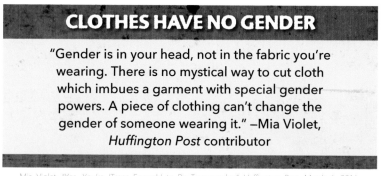

CLOTHES HAVE NO GENDER

"Gender is in your head, not in the fabric you're wearing. There is no mystical way to cut cloth which imbues a garment with special gender powers. A piece of clothing can't change the gender of someone wearing it." –Mia Violet, *Huffington Post* contributor

Mia Violet, "Yes, You're 'Trans Enough' to Be Transgender," *Huffington Post*, March 6, 2016. www.huffingtonpost.com/mia-violet/yes-youre-trans-enough-to_b_9318754.html.

Medical Transitioning

Medical transitioning involves making physical changes to one's body to better reflect one's gender identity. This can include hormone therapy, one or more surgeries, or a combination of the two. Hormone therapy uses hormones to help develop secondary sex characteristics that align with a person's gender identity and minimize the secondary sex characteristics that do not align with their gender identity. NCET defines gender-affirming surgeries as:

> Surgical procedures that change one's body to better reflect a person's gender identity. This may include different procedures, including those sometimes also referred to as "top surgery" (breast augmentation or removal) or "bottom surgery" (altering genitals). Contrary to popular belief, there is not one surgery; in fact there are many different surgeries. These surgeries are medically necessary for some people, however not all people want, need, or can have surgery as part of their transition.[99]

There is no one path to medical transitioning, and people choosing to pursue hormone therapy and gender-affirming surgery may undergo a process of trial and error before they are happy with the results of their treatment. For example, Sam Dylan Finch pointed out, "For non-binary folks, this delicate balance is even more challenging to achieve. Some of us end up back pedaling with our dose or coming off of hormones altogether, trying not to swing too hard in one direction of the binary or the other."[100]

Hormone Therapy

Estrogen is used in hormone therapy for people who want to develop secondary sex characteristics that society considers feminine. Through therapy, people will typically develop breasts, experience reduced muscle mass and body hair, change sweat and odor patterns, and possibly reverse hair loss.

A person who wants to start hormone therapy should talk to their doctor about the ways it will affect their body.

Currently, 17-beta estradiol is the most common class of estrogen used in this type of hormone therapy. It is bioidentical to the hormone that is naturally created in human ovaries. This helps people develop "feminine" secondary sex characteristics. People taking estrogen also often use testosterone blockers call antiandrogens, which work to minimize "masculine" secondary sex characteristics. Using anti-androgens allows people to take lower doses of estrogen.

People who want to develop "masculine" secondary sex characteristics and suppress "feminine" secondary sex characteristics can take hormone therapy involving testosterone. All of the testosterone preparations used in hormone therapy are bioidentical to the testosterone naturally produced inside human testicles. People who use this type of therapy will typically develop facial hair and increased body hair, experience vocal changes, gain muscle mass, change sweat and odor patterns, and possibly develop receding hairlines or baldness.

In both estrogen and testosterone hormone therapy, results happen gradually over time and differ from person to person. Mood swings are a common side effect of both types of therapy. Estrogen therapy can potentially lead to increased risk for blood clots, high blood pressure, or estrogen-related cancers. These risks can be monitored through blood tests and routine breast cancer screenings. Testosterone can potentially cause high cholesterol, blood clots, weight gain, and diabetes. On either type of therapy, consistent health screenings are helpful for avoiding these risks.

Gender-Affirming Surgery

There are different types of gender-affirming surgeries people can choose to pursue. Most gender-affirming surgeries affect the chest or genitals. Chest surgeries are often informally referred to as "top" surgeries, while genital surgeries are often called "bottom" surgeries. Not everyone who undergoes these surgeries may be comfortable with these terms.

Common chest surgeries include double mastectomy (breast removal) and breast augmentation surgeries (breast implants or adjustments made to breasts, such as increasing fullness and size). Common genital surgeries include neovaginoplasty (constructing a vulva and vagina), phalloplasty (constructing a penis), and metoidioplasty (constructing a penis from a clitoris enlarged by testosterone therapy).

Health Care

Affording health care and medical transition can be extremely difficult for transgender individuals. Many health insurance policies and programs exclude transgender people from equal access to the care they need. In 2011, a survey of more than 6,450 transgender individuals conducted by the National Center of Transgender Equality showed that 19 percent of participants were refused medical care because of their gender identity.

Medically transitioning is a necessity for many transgender individuals. Jillian Weiss, the executive director of the Transgender Legal Defense and Education fund, stated, "This is life-affirming and, in many cases, lifesaving treatment that is recognized as medically necessary by the medical profession."[101] Many organizations are pushing for equal health care for the transgender community, and there are laws currently in place to protect transgender individuals' rights to medical access. The Affordable Care Act prohibits discrimination based on gender identity, including refusing to cover an individual based on their gender identity or refusing to cover the costs of transition treatment. The Health Insurance Portability and Accountability Act also protects the privacy of transgender individuals' medical records, including their transition status. Still, much work needs to be done to ensure transgender individuals have access to the health care they need.

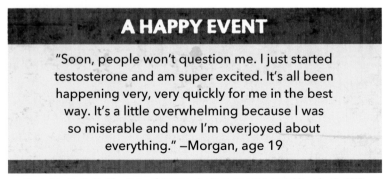

A HAPPY EVENT

"Soon, people won't question me. I just started testosterone and am super excited. It's all been happening very, very quickly for me in the best way. It's a little overwhelming because I was so miserable and now I'm overjoyed about everything." –Morgan, age 19

Quoted in David Yi, "The Faces of Transgender Teen America," Mashable, July 15, 2015. mashable.com/2015/08/31/transgender-teenagers/#2MZ4gdWPskqI.

Emotional Impact of Medically Transitioning

Choosing to medically transition is an extremely personal decision, and each person's experience is unique. In addition to side effects and bodily changes, medically transitioning can be an incredibly difficult emotional journey. Finch shared his personal struggle with hormone therapy: "I'm scrambling to find a space to just affirm that, yes, this is the best thing I've ever done and it's also the hardest thing I've ever been through."[102] Side effects and other personal health concerns such as mental illness can have a large impact on a person's experience of medically transitioning. Finch wrote, "This contradiction—that these hormones can be both life-giving and life-threatening—is impossibly hard to negotiate and is a testimony to just how complex this intersection of transness and mental illness can really be."[103] Seeking guidance from professional counselors who are well educated in transgender issues can be a crucial part of the transition process.

The permanence of surgeries can also be extremely intimidating. Some people may worry they will regret their decision, while others feel confident in their choice even before surgery. McConnell wrote about his decision to have chest surgery:

> Several people asked if I worried about taking such a big, non-reversible step in transition. No, I said, because when I imagined my future chest I felt happy, impatient and comforted all at once. My other, more pragmatic response was that, while I couldn't predict the future, I was absolutely certain my current situation was unsustainable.[104]

Choosing to medically transition or not to medically transition may be a long process. Ultimately, it is a personal choice and there is no right or wrong decision. Choosing either course of action does not at all impact whether or not a person is transgender, as one's gender identity does not rely on medical transition.

Changing the "Tragic" Narrative

Society often depicts physical transgender people as tragic figures. It downplays the actual difficulties and challenges transgender people face by reducing all their unique experiences into catch phrases such as "born in the wrong body." It also oversimplifies the transition process, often sensationalizing "before and after" photographs. This understanding of transitioning is both inaccurate and disrespectful.

Physically transitioning is almost always depicted by the media as a drastic, dramatic action. This is an unhelpful stereotype for the transgender community. Mia Violet wrote:

> You can transition without needing to. Transition doesn't have to be a desperate last resort. You can transition simply because you want to. Transition isn't a sacred act only for the worthy, it's for anyone that wants it. I'll let you in on a secret; only trans people want to transition. Only trans people size up how difficult transition is going to be and still think it looks enticing.[105]

Many people do feel an urgent need to transition, which is equally valid. The problem is that society often assumes there is a single "tragic" narrative that all trans people live. This stereotype lumps each person's unique experience into one story, which disrespects the real pain and difficulty trans people experience. In reality, each person has a unique situation, emotions, and reasons for wanting to transition.

Stereotypes and Expectations Rooted in the Gender Binary

Society often expects transgender people to express their gender in hyperfeminine or hypermasculine ways that fit neatly into the gender binary. Mia Violet wrote:

> Garbage documentaries love to force-feed the same tired narrative that trans women spend their days flipping through catalogues and crying over dresses, as if femininity is measured by how much you want to look like a 1980s Barbie doll. Meanwhile, trans men are similarly held to ridiculous standards, and non-binary people are erased altogether.[106]

This image of transgender people is harmful because it oversimplifies the complex relationship between gender identity and expression. Sam Dylan Finch explained, "The idea that transgender people must all 'present' a certain way is simply taking one oppressive idea of gender and replacing it with an equally oppressive and sexist one."[107]

The media's idea of a transgender person is often someone who is beautiful and androgynous. Some transgender people may fit this image, but not everyone does.

Transgender people often face more pressure to conform to the gender binary's stereotypes than cisgender people. Wiley Reading wrote:

Trans and genderqueer people are as complex and varied in their gender expression as non-trans people. We'd never tell Angelina Jolie that she's not a woman because she shaved her head or Hugh Jackman that he's not a man because he owns a tiny coat-wearing dog. So why do we police trans people's identities based on their aesthetic choices or the way their bodies look?[108]

"Passing"

"Passing" is a term which refers to how a person's gender expression reflects their gender identity, or how easy it is for others to "read" a person's gender. It is largely considered a deeply offensive term, especially because a person's gender identity does not at all rely on their gender expression. Yet it is important to recognize that the concept of "passing" influences the day-to-day lives of many transgender and nonbinary individuals. Not all transgender people want to "pass"—many are more comfortable expressing their gender in a way that does not fit neatly into society's ideas of feminine and masculine. However, members of the transgender community who do not "pass" as cisgender may face more harassment, discrimination, or discomfort in certain situations than those members of the transgender community who do "pass." Society's expectation that all people should express their gender in accordance with the gender binary is deeply harmful to the transgender community.

Amanda Stevens pointed out this double standard as well. She said, "We're having all these conversations on how women don't have to follow these strict lines of beauty. But when we look at trans people we go, 'No, but not you. If you don't follow the stereotypes, then how do I know you're a woman?'"[109]

Nonbinary and gender nonconforming people also often struggle with expectations of gender expression. Finch wrote about navigating nonbinary gender expression:

> When I was trying to get an idea of what I, as non-binary, wanted to look like, I couldn't help but notice that there was an abundance of thin, traditionally masculine, able-bodied white people without a single curve to be found that were being advertised as androgynous bodies.
>
> There weren't any bodies that looked like mine.
>
> But here's the truth: You can be fat and curvy and be androgynous. You can be a person of color and, undoubtedly, be neutrois. You can have [breasts] and be transmasculine.[110]

While a person may alter their gender expression or body to help them feel more in tune with their gender identity, their gender identity does not rely on a certain presentation.

CHAPTER 6

Challenges and Progress

The transgender community has seen some encouraging progress in the fight for its members' rights, especially in the last several years. Transgender, nonbinary, and gender nonconforming individuals have been largely erased from history. Today, the media is finally focusing on many transgender individuals and the issues the community as a whole faces. This is crucial because many transgender, nonbinary, and gender nonconforming people still face discrimination and the threat of violence in their everyday lives.

Citizens and politicians alike are pushing for laws that will help protect the transgender community and ensure their rights are protected. In addition to changing laws, society needs to eradicate its many forms of transphobia. From media coverage to conversation among friends, society needs to eliminate transphobic language and change its hateful attitude toward the transgender community.

Conversion Therapy

Conversion therapy is a practice dismissed by the majority of the medical and psychological community as unnecessary, unethical, and abusive. The practice involves "counselors" attempting to change a person's sexuality or gender identity, which can lead to devastating mental and emotional effects on LGBTQIA patients. Some parents of LGBTQIA youth force their children to undergo conversion therapy in order to "change" their sexuality to heterosexual or their gender identity to cisgender. Minors often cannot escape this abusive situation, and LGBTQIA and human rights organizations continue to fight on their behalf to ban conversion therapy all together.

Currently, conversion therapy is banned in California, Illinois, New Jersey, Oregon, Vermont, and the District of Columbia, and over 20 other states are introducing similar legislation. In states where conversion therapy is banned, licensed mental health providers can no longer offer conversion therapy to minors. In contrast, Oklahoma has introduced legislation that legally protects conversion therapy from state interference and legitimizes the practice.

Leelah's Law

In 2014, a transgender teen named Leelah Alcorn committed suicide by walking in front of a semitruck. Her suicide note, which she posted to Tumblr, explained that her parents had

Research on Suicide Attempts in the Transgender Community

In 2014, researchers from the Williams Institute and the American Foundation for Suicide Prevention found that certain groups of transgender and gender nonconforming individuals had particularly high rates of suicide attempts:

Listed Gender Identity
- 47 percent of transgender women surveyed
- 28 percent of transgender men surveyed
- 65 percent of participants who listed their identity as transgender

Age
- 45 percent of 18- to 24-year-olds (at some point in their lives)
- 45 percent of 25- to 44-year-olds (at some point in their lives)
- 39 percent of 45- to 54-year-olds (at some point in their lives)

Employment Status
- 20 percent of students
- 46 percent of full-time employees
- 65 percent of participants who experienced physical violence at work
- 64 percent of participants who were sexually assaulted at work

forced her to undergo Christian-based conversion therapy, withdrew her from public school, and isolated her from all forms of communication by taking away her laptop and cell phone.

Leelah's death and the objectionable actions of her parents sparked a call for federal action to ban conversion therapy across the nation. A petition titled Enact Leelah's Law to Ban All LGBTQIA Conversion Therapy collected more than 120,958 signatures. While a federal law would need to come from Congress, the White House responded with support for the petition, stating: "The overwhelming scientific evidence

- 59 percent of participants who were denied access to the appropriate bathrooms
- 56 percent of participants who were referred to by the wrong pronouns repeatedly and on purpose at work

Health Care Experiences

- 60 percent of participants who were denied treatment from a medical professional because of their gender identity
- 56 percent of participants who have avoided seeking medical help for illness of injury because of previous discrimination from medical professionals

Housing Experience

- 69 percent of participants who experienced homelessness
- 63 percent of participants who were evicted
- 62 percent of participants who had to move back in with family or friends

Experiences with Law Enforcement

- 70 percent of participants who were sexually assaulted by officers
- 60 percent of participants who were physically assaulted by officers
- 57 percent of participants who were generally disrespected by officers

demonstrates that conversion therapy, especially when it is practiced on young people, is neither medically nor ethically appropriate and can cause substantial harm."[111]

Mental Health

There is a misconception that simply being transgender causes mental health issues, but this is not at all the case. The immense pressure and discrimination that society exerts upon transgender individuals can negatively impact their mental health. The National Alliance on Mental Illness (NAMI) stated, "Often termed 'minority stress,' disparities in the LGBTQIA community stem from a variety of factors including social stigma, discrimination, prejudice, denial of civil and human rights, abuse, harassment, victimization, social exclusion and family rejection."[112] It is also completely possible for transgender people to experience mental health issues that are unrelated to their gender identity.

Mental health professionals who are educated on transgender issues can help individuals in many ways, such as:

- Exploring gender identity and learning self-acceptance
- Coping with gender dysphoria
- Coming out and socially transitioning
- Deciding whether or not to pursue medical transitioning and discussing medical transitioning options
- General mental health issues unrelated to a person's gender identity

Research suggests that accepting environments can have a positive effect on transgender individuals' mental health. In 2011, the National Transgender Discrimination Survey found that of the 6,450 transgender and gender nonconforming participants, 78 percent of participants were more

Society often creates a negative stigma around professional mental health services, but there is no shame in seeking professional help. These services are vital resources that help people cope with depression, anxiety, gender dysphoria, and countless other issues.

comfortable at work after transitioning. Likewise, a 2016 study titled "Mental Health of Transgender Children Who Are Supported in Their Identities" found that "Socially transitioned transgender children who are supported in their gender identity have developmentally normative levels of depression and only minimal elevations in anxiety, suggesting that psychopathology is not inevitable within this group."[113] This study shows that a supportive family and environment can have a tremendously positive effect on transgender youth.

Homelessness and Economic Discrimination

A disproportionate percent of the transgender community experiences housing discrimination or homelessness compared to the general population. NCET reports that one in five transgender individuals experiences homelessness at some point in their lifetime, and that LGBTQIA youth make up 20 to 40 percent of the 1.6 million homeless youth in the United States. In 2011, the National Transgender Discrimination Survey found that of the 6,450 transgender and gender nonconforming participants:

- 19 percent were refused a home or apartment
- 19 percent experienced homelessness in their lifetime because of their gender identity
- 11 percent were evicted from a residence because of their gender identity
- 55 percent were harassed by shelter staff or residents when seeking help
- 22 percent were sexually assaulted at a shelter by staff or residents
- 29 percent were denied service at a shelter
- 2 percent were homeless at the time of the survey (almost twice the rate of the general population)

Various forms of economic discrimination also severely impact the transgender community, which often contributes to the rates of homelessness. The survey found that:

- 50 percent of participants were harassed at work because of their gender identity
- 26 percent of participants lost a job because of their gender identity

- Participants who had lost a job because of their gender identity experienced homelessness at twice the rate of the general population, misused alcohol and drugs at a higher rate, were incarcerated at a higher rate, and had more than double the HIV infection rate
- People of color experienced up to four times the national unemployment rate
- 16 percent of participants were forced to turn to underground employment such as selling drugs

Many organizations seek to ensure equal housing for the LGBTQIA community, lessen the rates of homelessness among members of the LGBTQIA community, and eliminate discriminatory shelter policies. The U.S. Department of Housing and Urban Development currently protects transgender renters and homebuyers from discrimination based on their gender identities, but more work needs to be done to end transphobic practices.

Anti-Transgender Violence

The transgender community continues to experience many forms of violence, particularly against transgender women of color. Between 2013 and 2015, the Human Rights Coalition (HRC) recorded at least 53 transgender homicide victims, 46 of whom were transgender women of color. HRC also reported that 39 of the 53 victims were under the age of 35, which suggests transgender youth are especially at risk.

In 2015, the National Coalition of Anti-Violence Programs (NCAVP) received 1,976 reports of intimate partner violence against members of the LGBTQIA community and HIV-affected individuals. Of these reports, 10 percent of the survivors identified as transgender, 1 percent identified with a gender identity other than transgender or cisgender, and 1 percent identified as intersex. People of color made up the majority of intimate partner violence survivors (54 percent) and victims of intimate partner homicide (77 percent) reported to NCAVP. Out of 13 intimate partner homicides, 6 victims were transgender, and all 6 were transgender women of color.

Even institutions that help survivors of abuse continue to discriminate against the transgender community. The NCAVP

Transgender Day of Remembrance

In 1999, Gwendolyn Ann Smith founded the Transgender Day of Remembrance (TDOR) in honor of Rita Hester, a transgender woman who was killed in 1998. TDOR, which is held annually on November 20, is a vigil to commemorate those lost to anti-transgender violence while also raising awareness of crimes against the transgender community. Local transgender advocacy groups and LGBTQIA organizations across the country hold vigils in parks, places of worship, and other public places. Vigils generally include a reading of the list of names of the transgender individuals who were killed in acts of anti-transgender violence that year.

The LGBTQIA community and allies hold vigils on November 20 in honor of the transgender individuals who have lost their lives to acts of anti-transgender violence.

stated that of all the LGBTQIA and HIV-affected individuals who were denied assistance by shelters in 2015, 71 percent reported they were denied because of their gender identity. Transgender survivors are also more likely to experience certain types of harassment and violence than cisgender survivors. In 2015, the NCAVP found that transgender survivors were three times more likely to report stalking compared to cisgender survivors, and transgender women were three times more likely to report experiencing sexual and financial violence than cisgender survivors.

Government Action for Transgender Equality

In 2015, the Congressional LGBT Equality Caucus of the U.S. House of Representatives formed the Transgender Equality Task Force. On November 17, 2015, the Caucus held the first Congressional Forum on violence against the transgender community. Representative Michael Makoto Honda, who serves as the chair of the Transgender Equality Task Force, stated, "It is our responsibility as leaders and public officials to ensure that all people are free from the fear of persecution, prejudice, or violence just for being who they are. We work to highlight the issues that transgender individuals face."[114]

One of the Transgender Equality Task Force's main goals is to convince Congress to pass the Equality Act, which was proposed in 2015. If passed, this act would amend the Civil Rights Act of 1964 to explicitly prohibit discrimination against individuals based on sex, sexual orientation, and gender identity. This would ensure greater protections and freedoms for the LGBTQIA community, and would allow the Department of Justice to bring civil action against public, state, or federal facilities—such as restaurants, stores, and shelters—that deny individuals access or admission based on their sex, sexuality, or gender identity. The Customer Non-Discrimination Act, which is currently a bill, works to ensure similar protections in public spaces. The Equality Act would also amend the Fair Housing Act, the Equal Credit Opportunity Act, and jury selection standards to include sexuality and gender identity as classes that are protected from discrimination.

Under the Equality Act, employers with 15 or more employees would be prohibited from discriminating against their employees based on these factors. It also requires the employers to recognize and respect the sex, sexuality, and gender identity of their employees. The act would also update desegregation standards in schools to protect students from discrimination based on sex, sexuality, or gender identity. It would ensure everyone has access to shared spaces, such as restrooms and locker rooms, regardless of their sexuality or gender identity.

Anti-Transgender Government Action

Prejudice and transphobia continue to influence governmental action. The United States is home to starkly contrasting political beliefs, and the transgender community often finds itself in a political tug-of-war between progress toward civil rights and blatant discrimination. While many citizens and politicians advocate for transgender rights, many oppose transgender equality and push for discriminatory policies.

State and federal governments move back and forth between expanding transgender peoples' rights and eliminating them. Even when laws that support transgender equality are passed, they are sometimes repealed or altered. For example, GLAAD reported:

> In November 2015, residents of Houston, Texas, repealed the Houston Equal Rights Ordinance (HERO), which had previously afforded Houstonians protections on the basis of 15 characteristics, including sexual orientation and gender identity. Without laws such as this one, the transgender community will continue to face high rates of discrimination.[115]

The Public Facilities Privacy and Security Act

In addition to repealing transgender equality laws, conservative politicians continue to push forth anti-transgender laws that blatantly discriminate against the transgender community. In 2015, the North Carolina General Assembly passed the House Bill 2, "The Public Facilities Privacy and Security Act," which quickly became known in the media as the Bathroom Bill. The bill required public facilities and public schools to adopt a policy that forces transgender people to use the bathrooms and locker rooms that align with the sex listed on their birth certificate. It also prohibited cities and counties within North Carolina from creating their own non-discrimination laws that would protect LGB and transgender peoples' rights.

This action immediately put the civil rights and safety of transgender individuals in North Carolina at risk. Many transgender and nonbinary people feared that they would experience violence or harassment if they were forced to use the bathroom of the sex listed on their birth certificate. Preliminary results from the National Center of Transgender Equality's 2015 survey showed:

- 59 percent of transgender participants avoided using bathrooms in public out of fear of confrontation
- 31 percent avoided eating and drinking so they would not have to use the bathroom
- 24 percent were told they were using the wrong bathroom

- 9 percent were denied entry to the bathroom that aligns with their gender identity
- 12 percent were harassed, attacked, or sexually assaulted in a bathroom

The bill sparked outrage from the transgender community and allies, and Governor Pat McCrory immediately faced criticism for signing it into law. In May of 2016, the U.S. Justice Department filed a federal civil rights lawsuit to block The Public Facilities Privacy and Security Act in the hope that federal courts will find the bill unconstitutional. Unfortunately, this is just one example of the ongoing flux between pro-transgender equality laws and anti-transgender discrimination that leaves the transgender community vulnerable.

A Bull's-Eye for Change in the Business World

In the midst of the discriminatory bathroom legislation, Target publicly stated that transgender employees and shoppers are welcome to use whichever bathrooms and dressing rooms they feel comfortable in. In response, a conservative Christian group called the American Family Association started a boycott in protest of Target's inclusive policies. Rather than backing down, Target committed $20 million to creating gender-neutral bathrooms in all of its stores. So far, Target's stance on gender equality has been an enormous source of encouragement for the trans community.

Separate Bathrooms Are Not a Solution

Offering separate or private bathrooms is a great way to ensure anyone can feel comfortable when they go to the bathroom, whether or not they are transgender. However, private bathrooms may be unavailable or very inconvenient to access. More importantly, forcing transgender people to use private bathrooms when other people do not have to is isolating and reinforces the idea that transgender people are somehow harmful and should be kept separate from everybody else.

Target is making progress in other areas as well. The multibillion-dollar corporation will no longer divide certain departments by gender. So far, Target has committed to making toys and children's bedding completely gender-neutral. Instead of separating toys into girls' aisles and boys' aisles, there will be one gender-neutral toy department. The displays and shelves will not use colors that society associates with genders, such as pink, blue, and green. This will help move away from the idea that some toys are only for girls and others are only for boys. Kids will be able to look at all the toys without the pressure to stay in only one section. This could make it easier for kids to choose toys they are naturally interested in, rather than the toys they think they are "supposed to" play with.

In response to the Public Facilities Privacy and Security Act, some businesses marked their restrooms with gender-neutral signs.

While these may seem like small changes, Target has the potential to influence the way other businesses operate, and other corporations may follow Target's progressive footsteps and institute inclusive policies.

Representation in the Media

From the earliest childhood experiences and throughout a person's life, many of the messages received about gender come from the media. A crucial element to eliminating transphobia and discrimination against the transgender community is accurate, respectful representation of transgender individuals in the media. Without representation, the transgender community continues to be treated as "other" by the vast majority of society. Allowing transgender voices in the media will help address discrimination, inspire positive change, and normalize and embrace the transgender community as equal members of society.

While transgender representation has drastically increased and improved for the better in recent years, there is still much progress that needs to be made. Too often transgender and gender nonconforming characters in television and movies are punchlines to offensive jokes rooted in discrimination. Gender expression is heavily regulated by stereotypes rooted in the gender binary—a man wearing a dress is still seen as humorous or a form of humiliation rather than a valid form of expression. These messages continue to actively work against social progress for the transgender community. GLAAD explained:

> A recent Pew poll shows that 87% of Americans say they personally know someone who is lesbian, gay, or bisexual. If a stereotypical or defamatory LGB image appears in the media, viewers can compare it to real people they know. But when a stereotypical or defamatory transgender image appears in the media, the viewer may assume that all transgender people are actually like that; most have no real-life experience with which to compare it.[116]

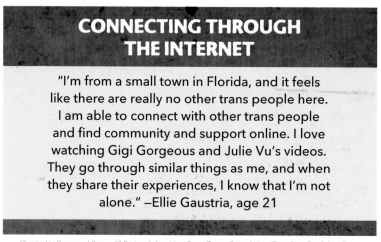

CONNECTING THROUGH THE INTERNET

"I'm from a small town in Florida, and it feels like there are really no other trans people here. I am able to connect with other trans people and find community and support online. I love watching Gigi Gorgeous and Julie Vu's videos. They go through similar things as me, and when they share their experiences, I know that I'm not alone." –Ellie Gaustria, age 21

Quoted in Raymond Braun, "7 Seriously Inspiring Trans Teens Reveal How They Stay Confident Even When People Try to Knock Them Down," *Seventeen*, December 30, 2015. www.seventeen.com/life/g2679/self-confidence-tips-transgender-teens/?slide=4.

Without genuine representation, the cisgender majority of society will continue to believe stereotypes about the transgender community rather than respecting transgender individuals. Fortunately, more and more transgender, nonbinary, and gender nonconforming individuals are finally receiving platforms to speak.

Changing the World

The following members of the transgender community have changed the world and fought for transgender rights and representation.

Geraldine Roman became the first transgender Congresswoman in the Philippines in 2016, winning an impressive 62 percent of the vote. Her achievement is a victory for the LGBTQIA community, particularly in light of the strong conservative Catholic presence that often creates hostility towards LGBTQIA individuals in the Philippines.

Geraldine Roman is shown here introducing herself to a voter.

Janet Mock is a successful Hawaiian writer, TV host, advocate for the transgender community, and founder of #GirlsLikeUs—a social media movement that empowers transgender women. Her memoir, *Redefining Realness: My Path to Womanhood, Identity, Love & So Much More*, was a New York Times Bestseller that movingly raised awareness of many transgender issues. She also produced and conducted all of the interviews for an HBO documentary called *The Trans List*, and continues to push for transgender representation in the media.

Laverne Cox plays Sophia Burset on Netflix's *Orange Is the New Black*. She is the first transgender woman of color to play a leading role on a mainstream scripted television show and the first openly transgender person to ever be nominated

Laverne Cox is famous for her role in Orange Is the New Black.

for an Emmy. Cox is also renowned for her eloquent, moving speeches about transgender issues, sexism, and racism.

Ian Harvie is a talented comedian who began his career opening for Margaret Cho. In 2013, he released his first live stand-up film performance, *Ian Harvie Superhero.* He brings his personal experiences as a transgender man, from his gender-affirming surgery to fear of public bathrooms, into his humor. His work addresses important transgender issues while creating an atmosphere of acceptance.

Jaiyah Saelua identifies as Fa'afafine, which in Samoan culture is someone who is born with sex characteristics that are considered male, but who embodies both masculinity and femininity. Saelua was the first transgender national soccer player to compete in a men's FIFA World Cup for American Samoa in 2011.

Creating Positive Change

There is still much that needs to be done to end discrimination based on gender identity and expression and to ensure equal, protected rights for members of the transgender community and intersex individuals. Combating society's ignorance through educating the public with accurate information about sex and gender identity (that is not clouded by prejudice) is an essential step in this process. As transgender, nonbinary, gender nonconforming, and intersex individuals become increasingly visible in the mainstream media, society has the opportunity to listen to their voices and change for the better. As a nation, there is a need to collectively strive to create a society that embraces differences rather than fearing them, pass laws to protect the transgender community and intersex individuals rather than laws that actively discriminate against them, and allow everyone to express their authentic selves without fear.

Chapter 1: What Is Sex?

1. "Physical Development in Boys: What to Expect," The American Academy of Pediatrics, November 21, 2015. www.healthychildren.org/English/ages-stages/gradeschool/puberty/Pages/Physical-Development-Boys-What-to-Expect.aspx.

2. "Answers to Your Questions About Individuals With Intersex Conditions," Amercican Psychological Association, 2016. www.apa.org/topics/lgbt/intersex.aspx

3. "Fact Sheet Intersex," Free & Equal United Nations for LGBT Equality. unfe.org/system/unfe-65-Intersex_Factsheet_ENGLISH.pdf.

4. "What Is Intersex?," Intersex Society of North America. www.isna.org/faq/what_is_intersex.

5. "INTERSEX!," YouTube video, 4:48, posted by lacigreen, December 10, 2015. www.youtube.com/watch?v=4IJyHxQH2eY.

6. Claudia, "Claudia Is Intersex, Let's Talk About It," Autostraddle, February 20, 2013. www.autostraddle.com/claudia-is-intersex-lets-talk-about-it-149137/.

7. "What's It Like to be Intersex?," YouTube video, 3:25, posted by BuzzFeedYellow, March 28, 2015. www.youtube.com/watch?v=cAUDKEI4QKI.

8. "What's It Like to be Intersex?," YouTube video, posted by BuzzFeedYellow.

9. "What's It Like to be Intersex?," YouTube video, posted by BuzzFeedYellow.

10. "What's It Like to be Intersex?," YouTube video, posted by BuzzFeedYellow.

11. "What's It Like to be Intersex?," YouTube video, posted by BuzzFeedYellow.

12. "Does ISNA Think Children with Intersex Should Be Raised Without a Gender, or in a Third Gender?," Intersex Society of North America. www.isna.org/faq/third-gender.

13. "What's It Like to be Intersex?," YouTube video, posted by BuzzFeedYellow.

14. "Understanding Gender," Gender Spectrum. www.genderspectrum.org/quick-links/understanding-gender/.

15. Adrian Ballou, "Boy, Girl, Neither, Both? Why Assuming Is Awkward (And What to Ask Instead)," *Everyday Feminism*, 2016. everydayfeminism.com/2015/05/assuming-gender/.

Chapter 2: What Is Gender?

16. *Merriam-Webster Online*, s.vv. "social construct". www.merriam-webster.com/dictionary/social%20construct.

17. Wiley Reading, "Separating Out Gender Identity from Gender Expression," *Everyday Feminism*, May 15, 2014. everydayfeminism.com/2014/05/separating-identity-expression/.

18. "Transgender Terminology," National Center for Transgender Equality, January 15, 2014. www.transequality.org/issues/resources/transgender-terminology.

19. "LGBTQ+ Definitions," Trans Student Educational Resources, 2016. www.transstudent.org/definitions.

20. "GLAAD Media Reference Guide—Transgender," GLAAD, 2016. www.glaad.org/reference/transgender.

21. "Terminology—Gender Diversity," Gender Diversity, 2016. www.genderdiversity.org/resources/terminology/.

22. Jessie Mooney, "OITNB's Ruby Rose Schools Us on Gender Fluidity," *ELLE*, June 15, 2015. www.elle.com/culture/movies-tv/a28865/ruby-rose-oitnb/.

23. Jayson Flores, "How It Feels to Date When You're Bigender," Gay Pride—LGBT & Queer Voices, April 14, 2016. www.pride.com/dating/2016/4/14/how-it-feels-date-when-youre-bigender.

24. Flores, "How It Feels to Date When You're Bigender."

25. "LGBTQ+ Definitions," Trans Student Educational Resources.

26. "What Is Neutrois?," Neutrois.com, 2016. neutrois.com/what-is-neutrois/.

27. Sunnivie Brydum, "The True Meaning of the Word 'Cisgender,'" *Advocate,* July 31, 2015. www.advocate.com/transgender/2015/07/31/true-meaning-word-cisgender.

28. Sam Dylan Finch, "130 Examples Of Cis Privilege in All Areas of Life For You To Reflect On and Address," *Everyday Feminism,* February 29, 2016. everydayfeminism.com/2016/02/130-examples-cis-privilege/.

29. Finch, "130 Examples Of Cis Privilege in All Areas of Life For You To Reflect On and Address."

30. "LGBTQ+ Definitions," Trans Student Educational Resources.

31. Chelsea Yarborough, "7 Ways You Can Use Your Cisgender Privilege for Good," Feminist Campus, November 30, 2015. feministcampus.org/7-ways-you-can-use-your-cisgender-privilege-for-good/.

32. JR Thorpe, "11 Ways To Be A Trans* Ally, According To Transgender People Themselves," Bustle. www.bustle.com/articles/76762-11-ways-to-be-a-trans-ally-according-to-transgender-people-themselves.

33. Yarborough, "7 Ways You Can Use Your Cisgender Privilege for Good."

34. Reading, "Separating Out Gender Identity from Gender Expression."

35. Adrian Ballou, "10 Myths About Non-Binary People It's Time to Unlearn," *Everyday Feminism,* December 6, 2014. everydayfeminism.com/2014/12/myths-non-binary-people/.

Chapter 3: Navigating Gender Identity

36. Reading, "Separating Out Gender Identity from Gender Expression."

37. Reading, "Separating Out Gender Identity from Gender Expression."

38. "Gender Identity Development in Children," The American Academy of Pediatrics, November 21, 2015. www.healthychildren.org/English/ages-stages/gradeschool/Pages/Gender-Identity-and-Gender-Confusion-In-Children.aspx.

39. "Gender Non-Conforming & Transgender Children," The American Academy of Pediatrics, November 21, 2015. www.healthy-children.org/English/ages-stages/gradeschool/Pages/Gender-Non-Conforming-Transgender-Children.aspx.

40. Quoted in German Lopez, "9 Transgender People Talk about When They Knew, Coming Out, and Finding Love," *Vox*, April 23, 2015. www.vox.com/a/transgender-stories.

41. Quoted in Lopez, "9 Transgender People Talk about When They Knew, Coming Out, and Finding Love."

42. Quoted in Zosia Bielski, "Growing up Trans: Six Teens Open up about Discovering Who They Really Are," *The Globe and Mail*, July 17, 2015. www.theglobeandmail.com/life/growing-up-trans-six-teens-open-up-about-discovering-who-they-really-are/article25527446/.

43. Bielski, "Growing up Trans: Six Teens Open up about Discovering Who They Really Are."

44. Quoted in Lopez, "9 Transgender People Talk about When They Knew, Coming Out, and Finding Love."

45. Quoted in Lopez, "9 Transgender People Talk about When They Knew, Coming Out, and Finding Love."

46. Sam Dylan Finch, "8 Things Non-Binary People Need to Know." Let's Queer Things Up!, March 15, 2015. letsqueerthingsup.com/2015/03/15/8-things-non-binary-people-need-to-know/.

47. Mia Violet, "Yes, You're 'Trans Enough' to Be Transgender," *Huffington Post*, March 6, 2016. www.huffingtonpost.com/mia-violet/yes-youre-trans-enough-to_b_9318754.html.

48. Sam Dylan Finch, "5 Totally Normal Questions Transgender People May Be Afraid to Ask, Answered," *Everyday Feminism*, February 17, 2016. everydayfeminism.com/2016/02/questions-trans-people-have/.

49. Violet, "Yes, You're 'Trans Enough' to Be Transgender."

50. Quoted in Lopez, "9 Transgender People Talk about When They Knew, Coming Out, and Finding Love."

51. Sam Dylan Finch, "8 Tips for Coming Out as Non-Binary," *Everyday Feminism*, July 29, 2015. everydayfeminism.com/2015/07/coming-out-as-non-binary/.

52. "I Think I Might Be Transgender, Now What Do I Do?," Advocates for Youth, 2008. www.advocatesforyouth.org/publications/ publications-a-z/731-i-think-i-might-be-transgender-now-what-do-i-do.

53. "Tips for Allies of Transgender People," GLAAD, May 2015. www.glaad.org/transgender/allies.

54. Quoted in Lopez, "9 Transgender People Talk about When They Knew, Coming Out, and Finding Love."

55. Quoted in Lopez, "9 Transgender People Talk about When They Knew, Coming Out, and Finding Love."

Chapter 4: Finding the Right Language

56. "Why Pronouns Matter for Trans People," YouTube video, 2:29, posted by BuzzFeedYellow, March 16, 2015. www.youtube.com/ watch?v=N_yBGQqg7kM.

57. "Finding the Gender Pronoun That's Right for You," ReachOut. us.reachout.com/facts/factsheet/finding-the-gender-pronoun-thats-right-for-you.

58. "Why Pronouns are Important to Trans People," YouTube video, 5:01, posted by Kat Blaque, March 28, 2015. www.youtube.com/ watch?v=WXWmv1-4xFg.

59. "Why Pronouns Matter for Trans People," YouTube video, posted by BuzzFeedYellow.

60. "Why Pronouns Matter for Trans People," YouTube video, posted by BuzzFeedYellow.

61. "Why Pronouns are Important to Trans People," YouTube video, posted by Kat Blaque.

62. Joli St. Patrick, "What You're Really Saying When You Misgender," *The Body Is Not An Apology*, June 27, 2015. thebodyisnotanapology.com/magazine/what-youre-really-saying-when-you-misgender/.

63. Quoted in Petey Gibson, "Why Asking Someone What Gender Pronoun They Use Is So Important," *TeenVogue*, March 2, 2016. www.teenvogue.com/story/gender-pronouns.

64. Petey Gibson, "Why Asking Someone What Gender Pronoun They Use Is So Important."

65. West Anderson, "Pronoun Round Etiquette: How to Create Spaces That Are More Inclusive," *The Body Is Not An Apology*, October 22, 2016. thebodyisnotanapology.com/magazine/pronoun-round-etiquette/.

66. West Anderson, "Pronoun Round Etiquette: How to Create Spaces That Are More Inclusive."

67. Amanda Stevens, video interview by author, September 24, 2016.

68. "Why Pronouns Matter for Trans People," YouTube video, posted by BuzzFeedYellow.

69. Quoted in Lopez, "9 Transgender People Talk about When They Knew, Coming Out, and Finding Love."

70. West Anderson, "Pronouns and Misgendering," *The Body Is Not An Apology*, December 2, 2014. thebodyisnotanapology.com/magazine/pronouns-and-misgendering/.

71. "What if I Make a Mistake?," University of Wisconsin-Milwaukee LGBT Resource Center, 2016. uwm.edu/lgbtrc/qa_faqs/what-if-i-make-a-mistake/.

72. Anderson, "Pronouns and Misgendering."

73. Sam Dylan Finch, "What You're Actually Saying When You Ignore Someone's Gender Pronouns," Let's Queer Things Up!, September 15, 2014. letsqueerthingsup.com/2014/09/15/what-youre-actually-saying-when-you-ignore-someones-preferred-gender-pronouns/.

74. Quoted in Melissa Dahl, "How Transgender People Choose Their New Names," Science of Us, June 3, 2015. nymag.com/scienceofus/2015/06/how-transgender-people-choose-their-new-names.html.

75. Fred McConnell, "Trans Life: How I Plucked My New Name from the Family Tree," *The Guardian*, May 14, 2015. www.theguardian.com/lifeandstyle/2015/may/14/trans-life-name-family-tree-transition-ancestral-links.

76. Fred McConnell, "Trans Life: How I Plucked My New Name from the Family Tree."

77. Quoted in Sarah Karlan, "We Asked Trans People to Share the Stories of Their Names," BuzzFeed, March 1, 2016. www.buzzfeed.com/skarlan/we-asked-trans-people-to-share-the-unique-stories-behind-the?utm_term=.vnq5gq2qz7#.saGnm4O4zd.

78. "FTM Transgender: How I Chose My Name," YouTube video, 1:42, posted by Jammidodger, October 7, 2015. www.youtube.com/watch?v=4Vdz8sZhYoM&t=9s.

79. Silas Hansen, "Blank Slate," *Colorado Review*, Spring 2013. coloradoreview.colostate.edu/features/blank-slate/.

80. Quoted in Sarah Karlan, "We Asked Trans People to Share the Stories of Their Names."

81. Hansen, "Blank Slate."

82. Hansen, "Blank Slate."

Chapter 5: Gender Expression and Transitioning

83. "Gender Dysphoria," American Psychiatric Association, February 2016. www.psychiatry.org/patients-families/gender-dysphoria.

84. Zinnia Jones, "'That Was Dysphoria?' 8 Signs and Symptoms of Indirect Gender Dysphoria," The Orbit, September 10, 2013. the-orbit.net/zinniajones/2013/09/that-was-dysphoria-8-signs-and-symptoms-of-indirect-gender-dysphoria/.

85. "GLAAD Media Reference Guide—Transgender," GLAAD.

86. Quoted in Sarah Karlan, "We Asked People to Illustrate Their Gender Dysphoria," BuzzFeed, May 10, 2016. www.buzzfeed.com/skarlan/we-asked-people-to-illustrate-what-their-gender-dysphoria-fe?utm_term=.yyp29MDMr3#.gfWb2DgDwB.

87. Quoted in Karlan, "We Asked People to Illustrate Their Gender Dysphoria."

88. Stevens, video interview by author.

89. Stevens, video interview by author.

90. Jenny Crofton, "9 Strategies for Dealing with Gender Dysphoria for Gender Queer and Trans Folks," *The Body is Not an Apology*, November 15, 2016. thebodyisnotanapology.com/magazine/9-strategies-for-dealing-with-body-dysphoria-for-gender-queer-and-trans-folks/.

91. Crofton, "9 Strategies for Dealing with Gender Dysphoria for Gender Queer and Trans Folks."

92. "Packing," Provincial Health Services Authority, 2016. transhealth.phsa.ca/social-transition-options/binding-packing-tucking/what-is-packing.

93. "Tucking," Provincial Health Services Authority, 2016. transhealth.phsa.ca/social-transition-options/binding-packing-tucking/tucking.

94. Meredith Talusan, "All The Questions You Had About Tucking, But Were Afraid To Ask," BuzzFeed, April 2, 2016. www.buzzfeed.com/meredithtalusan/all-the-questions-you-had-about-tucking-but-were-afraid-to-a?utm_term=.irO37NANLe#.vqrlyn8nxm.

95. "Padding," Provincial Health Services Authority, 2016. transhealth.phsa.ca/social-transition-options/binding-packing-tucking/padding.

96. "Binding," Provincial Health Services Authority, 2016. transhealth.phsa.ca/social-transition-options/binding-packing-tucking/binding.

97. Meg Zulch, "7 Things You Should Know Before Buying Your First Chest Binder," Bustle, February 23, 2016. www.bustle.com/articles/138935-7-things-you-should-know-before-buying-your-first-chest-binder.

98. "GLAAD Media Reference Guide—Transgender," GLAAD.

99. "Transgender Terminology," National Center for Transgender Equality.

100. Sam Dylan Finch, "Am I the Only Transgender Person Sick of Transitioning?," Let's Queer Things Up!, August 13, 2016. letsqueerthingsup.com/2016/08/13/am-i-the-only-transgender-person-sick-of-transitioning/.

101. Quoted in Dawn Ennis, "More U.S. Hospitals Offering Gender-affirming Surgeries," NBCNews.com, October 31, 2016. www.nbcnews.com/feature/nbc-out/more-u-s-hospitals-offer-gender-affirming-surgeries-n674436.

102. Sam Dylan Finch, "Medically Transitioning Is Not A Walk In The Park (Sometimes, It Actually Sucks)," Let's Queer Things Up!, March 21, 2016. letsqueerthingsup.com/2016/03/21/medically-transitioning-is-not-a-walk-in-the-park/.

103. Finch, "Medically Transitioning Is Not A Walk In The Park (Sometimes, It Actually Sucks)."

104. Fred McConnell, "The Gift of a Lifetime: How Trans 'Top Surgery' Changed My Life," *The Guardian*, June 30, 2014. www.theguardian.com/society/2014/jun/30/trans-top-surgery-changed-my-life.

105. Violet, "Yes, You're 'Trans Enough' to Be Transgender."

106. Violet, "Yes, You're 'Trans Enough' to Be Transgender."

107. Sam Dylan Finch, "I Am Transgender, and I Am 'Trans Enough,'" Let's Queer Things Up!, November 14, 2014. letsqueerthingsup.com/2014/11/14/i-am-transgender-and-i-am-trans-enough/.

108. Reading, "Separating Out Gender Identity from Gender Expression."

109. Stevens, video interview by author.

110. Finch, "8 Things Non-Binary People Need to Know."

Chapter 6: Challenges and Progress

111. Valerie Jarrett, "Response to Your Petition on Conversion Therapy," We the People, 2015. petitions.whitehouse.gov/petition/enact-leelahs-law-ban-all-lgbtq-conversion-therapy.

112. "LGBTQ," The National Alliance on Mental Illness, 2016. www.nami.org/Find-Support/LGBTQ.

113. Kristina Olson, Lily Durwood, Madeleine DeMeules, and Katie McLaughlin, "Mental Health of Transgender Children Who Are Supported in Their Identities," AAP News & Journals Gateway, 2014. pediatrics.aappublications.org/content/early/2016/02/24/peds.2015-3223.

114. Jennifer Pike Bailey, "Congressional LGBT Equality Caucus Announces Transgender Equality Task Force," Human Rights Campaign, November 17, 2015. www.hrc.org/blog/congressional-lgbt-equality-caucus-announces-transgender-equality-task-forc.

115. "The 2016 Election: Know the Facts about Transgender People," GLAAD, 2016. www.glaad.org/vote/topics/transgender-people.

116. "The 2016 Election: Know the Facts about Transgender People," GLAAD.

Chapter 1: What Is Sex?

1. How have society's misconceptions about sex influenced its ideas about gender?

2. Why is it scientifically inaccurate to think of sex as a binary?

3. What are some of the ethical concerns that lead people to protest medically unnecessary genital surgeries for infants and children?

Chapter 2: What Is Gender?

1. How have you witnessed or experienced gender roles in your own life?

2. What are some of the different ways children learn about gender roles from an early age?

3. Which current theory of gender makes the most sense to you? Do you have your own way of thinking about gender?

Chapter 3: Navigating Gender Identity

1. Why is it culturally inappropriate for a non-Native American to describe themselves as Two Spirit?

2. How is gender expression different from gender identity?

3. Why is it harmful to question whether someone is "trans enough"?

Chapter 4: Finding the Right Language

1. What are some other gender-neutral pronouns people can use besides "they"?

2. Where do you notice unnecessarily gendered language in your daily life? What are some alternative words or phrases you and those around you could use instead?

3. How could you make introducing pronouns part of your school environment? What policies could your school adopt to make it easier for individuals to choose their name and pronouns?

Chapter 5: Gender Expression and Transitioning

1. Why is the "tragic" transgender narrative a harmful stereotype to the transgender community?

2. What are some of the steps a person can take to ensure they are binding safely?

3. How could you offer support to a friend or family member struggling with gender dysphoria? What resources would you suggest to them?

Chapter 6: Challenges and Progress

1. What are some ways a business could ensure its employees and customers feel safe expressing their gender identity?

2. Why is positive representation in the media important? How is it beneficial to the transgender community specifically?

3. #GirlsLikeUs is an empowering tool for transgender women to form an online community. What are some ways social media could create positive change in the transgender community?

Black Trans Advocacy
3530 Forest Lane, Suite 38
Dallas, TX 75234
Phone: (855) 255-8636
Website: www.blacktrans.org
Black Trans Advocacy is a national social justice organization that seeks to end violence and discrimination. It works in communities in the United States and the rest of the world to educate the public and push for progressive laws and policies.

COLAGE
3815 S. Othello Street, Suite 100, #310
Seattle, WA 98118
Phone: (855) 426-5243 (855-4-COLAGE)
E-mail: colage@colage.org
Website: www.colage.org
COLAGE is a network of youth ages 8 to 18 with LGBTQIA parents. It seeks to create a community that empowers and inspires its members and values social justice.

InterACT Advocates for Intersex Youth
365 Boston Post Road, Suite 163
Sudbury, MA 01776
Phone: (707) 793-1190
Website: interactadvocates.org
InterACT Advocates for Intersex Youth is an organization dedicated to raising awareness of intersex issues, empowering young intersex activists, and advocating for laws and policies that protect intersex youth. Members build a sense of community through a private Facebook group, Google Hangout video chats, and the organization's Tumblr.

The National Suicide Prevention Lifeline
Phone: (800) 273-8255 (800-273-TALK)
Website: suicidepreventionlifeline.org
This service provides free, confidential crisis support for anyone who

is considering suicide for any reason. A live chat is also available through the website.

Trans Lifeline
2443 Fillmore St
#380-9468
San Francisco, CA 94115
Phone: (877) 565-8860
Website: www.translifeline.org
This nonprofit organization is staffed by transgender people, so they are uniquely able to understand the issues other transgender people face. The goal of the organization is to help transgender people who are considering harming themselves, but they welcome anyone who feels overwhelmed to call.

The Trevor Project
P.O. Box 69232
West Hollywood, CA 90069
Phone (Lifeline): (866) 488-7386
Text: (202) 304-1200
Website: www.thetrevorproject.org
The Trevor Project is a nonprofit organization that provides resources for LGBTQIA people aged 13 to 24 who are considering self-harm or suicide. The Lifeline is available 24 hours a day, 7 days a week for people who need to talk to a crisis intervention counselor immediately. A live chat is available on the website every day between 3:00 p.m. and 9:00 p.m. Eastern Standard Time (EST), and counselors are available via text on Thursdays and Fridays between 4:00 p.m. and 8:00 p.m. EST.

Trans Youth Equality Foundation
P.O. Box 7441
Portland, ME 04112
Phone: (207) 478-4087
Website: www.transyouthequality.org.
The Trans Youth Equality Foundation is a nonprofit organization that advocates for transgender, gender nonconforming, and intersex children and young adults ages 2 to 18. They offer annual retreats including summer and fall camps, host an educational podcast titled TransWaves, and train educational and medical professionals on transgender issues.

Books

Andrews, Arin. *Some Assembly Required: The Not-So-Secret Life of a Transgender Teen*. New York, NY: Simon & Schuster BFYR, 2014.
This memoir details Andrews's experience with gender reassignment in high school, from the reasons he chose to undergo reassignment to the reactions he faced from others as a result of his decision.

Kuklin, Susan. *Beyond Magenta: Transgender Teens Speak Out*. Somerville, MA: Candlewick Press, 2014.
Interviews with six transgender and gender-neutral teens show that issues surrounding gender affect everyone differently. Things such as family life, living situation, and geographical location can have a huge effect on how a person comes to terms with their gender identity.

Pelleschi, Andrea, and Amy Stone. *Transgender Rights and Issues*. Minneapolis, MN: Essential Library, 2016.
Although Western society has come a long way in recognizing the rights and struggles of transgender people, there is still a long way to go. The situation is even worse in some other countries. Learning about the progress that still must be made can make people better informed about ways to fight for transgender rights.

Prince, Liz. *Tomboy: A Graphic Memoir*. San Francisco, CA: Zest Books, 2014.
Told in a graphic novel format, Prince details her struggle to find her place in a world that seemed intent on assigning her specific roles based on her gender.

Testa, Rylan Jay, Deborah Coolhart, and Jayme Peta. *The Gender Quest Workbook: A Guide for Teens and Young Adults Exploring Gender Identity*. Oakland, CA: Instant Help Books, 2015.
This workbook helps transgender teens cope with the issues they may face as a result of their search for their identity. Using worksheets and skills from cognitive behavioral therapy (CBT) and other types of therapy, teens can learn healthy ways to deal with anxiety, depression, and isolation. They can also learn how to navigate social situations and

make their needs and wants known in the most effective way.

Websites

The Center for Excellence for Transgender Health (CoE)
transhealth.ucsf.edu/trans?page=lib-providers
The CoE provides access to and information on the health care needs of transgender individuals. It strives to unite the Pacific AIDs Education and Training Center with the Center for AIDS Prevention Studies.

Gender Spectrum
www.genderspectrum.org/
Gender Spectrum works to create a world that is accepting of people of all gender identities through education. It helps spread awareness and understanding of transgender and gender-expansive issues. The website offers easy-to-understand information on the basics of gender identity.

GLAAD
www.glaad.org/transgender/resources
GLAAD lists a number of crucial transgender resources, including transgender suicide hotlines, transgender organizations, transgender specific programs hosted by LGBTQIA organizations, and general information.

The National Center for Transgender Equality (NCET)
www.transequality.org/
NCET is the leading social justice advocacy organization for the transgender community in the United States. It seeks to end discrimination and violence against the transgender community, promote beneficial laws and policies, and to educate the public on transgender issues.

TransLatin@ Coalition
Website: www.translatinacoalition.org.
TransLatin@ Coalition advocates for the specific needs of the transgender Latin@ community in the United States. The coalition seeks to educate the public and empower transgender leaders.

Trans Student Educational Resources (TSER)
www.transstudent.org/
TSER is a youth-run organization that works to create inclusive educational environments for transgender and gender nonconforming students. Its mission is to educate the public and give trans activists the tools they need to effect change.

INDEX

PICTURE CREDITS

Cover (top) UTBP/Shutterstock.com; cover (bottom) BestPhotoStudio/Shutterstock.com; p. 11 somersault1824/Shutterstock.com; p. 21 Marc Romanelli/Getty Images; p. 24 © iStockphoto.com/igorovski; p. 27 John Lamparski/WireImage/Getty Images; p. 28 Brendon Thorne/Getty Images for Paramount Pictures; p. 35 ekler/Shutterstock.com; p. 37 Henk Meyers/EyeEm/EyeEm Premium/Getty Images; p. 42 Jupiterimages/Photolibrary/Getty Images; p. 49 JGI/Jamie Grill/Blend Images/Getty Images; p. 54 Helga Esteb/Shutterstock.com; p. 59 Marie Killen/Moment/Getty Images; p. 60 Gina Kelly/Alamy Stock Photo; p. 62 Barcroft/Barcroft Media/Getty Images; p. 64 © iStockphoto.com/sturti; p. 69 zadirako/Shutterstock.com; p. 74 KatarzynaBialasiewicz/iStock/Thinkstock; p. 77 HECTOR MATA/AFP/Getty Images; p. 81 John Arehart/Shutterstock.com; p. 83 TED ALJIBE/AFP/Getty Images; p. 84 Nicholas Hunt/Getty Images Fragrance Foundation.

ABOUT THE AUTHOR

Kate Light is an editor of children's nonfiction and a freelance writer. She uses her passion for children's literature to help create progressive, educational books. She graduated from Canisius College with a Bachelor's degree in English and creative writing. As a cisgender woman, Kate experiences gender privilege and has a limited perspective of the issues transgender, nonbinary, gender nonconforming, and intersex people face. She cares deeply about social justice and LGBTQIA issues and hopes the research she has conducted for this book will help educate readers.

Special thanks to Amanda Stevens for agreeing to be interviewed for this book, and to Michael Sciandra and Michelle Denton for their invaluable contributions to this book.